There and Back

There and Back

Pennine walks between
Hebden Bridge and Todmorden

ISBN 0 9510790 2 6

Also by the same Author:
On the tops around Todmorden,
Short Walks for Motorists.

Published by Delta G
The Mistal, Butts Lane
TODMORDEN, OL14 8RJ

Text prepared by the Author using Microsoft Word.
Text transferred and page set by the printers:

Arc and Throstle Press, Nanholme Mill, Todmorden

Cover photograph: Stoodley Pike, from Bald Scout Hill,
showing the Pennine Way and Long Stoop.

There and Back

Pennine Walks between Hebden Bridge and Todmorden

by

GEOFF BOSWELL

Delta G
Todmorden

Contents

Walks from Todmorden to Hebden Bridge

Photographs

Introduction

A good walk is part of the good life. People who keep active to fight the flab often live to a ripe old age. The people of Calderdale have been walking the beautiful countryside around Todmorden and Hebden Bridge for years. There have been many books of walks dedicated to the area, the pioneers being "Pennine Walks around Hebden Bridge" and "On the Tops around Todmorden". Other books, which have followed them, are listed in the bibliography. These two country towns are just four and a half miles apart. You can walk from one to the other along the canal bank in just a little over an hour and yet they have retained their separate identities to this day. Walks have tended to be centred on one town or the other rather than on the countryside between them.

Hebden Bridge was once a wool town but following the decline of the textile industry a few far sighted local people started Pennine Heritage which breathed new life into the town, so much so that it has become a tourist hot spot. Writers and artists make use of the Hebden Bridge net site (http://www. hebdenbridge.co.uk/) while filmmakers often make use of the locations in and around the town.

Todmorden was a cotton town, where the decline of the cotton industry was slower. Indeed Todmorden retains some textile firms in manufacturing, bleaching and dying. New industries have come in. Tourism has developed - largely following local initiatives in setting up the Todmorden Information Centre Trust. New public buildings such as the Health Centre, the bus station and two new supermarkets have brightened up the town although this has put pressure on the small shops and the market. Yet Todmorden Market remains a buyer's paradise.

The two towns tend to be self-sufficient; they even have their own newspapers. Calderdale has its centre of local government in Halifax, which is remote, as far as the citizens of the two towns are concerned. Yet the Calderdale Countryside Service has an excellent reputation in providing for the needs of walkers in the area.

This book is designed to open up the countryside routes between the two towns. All the walks go from one to the other. You can go there by one route and back by another. All the walks interconnect at both Todmorden and Hebden Bridge. If you happen to live between the two towns or be

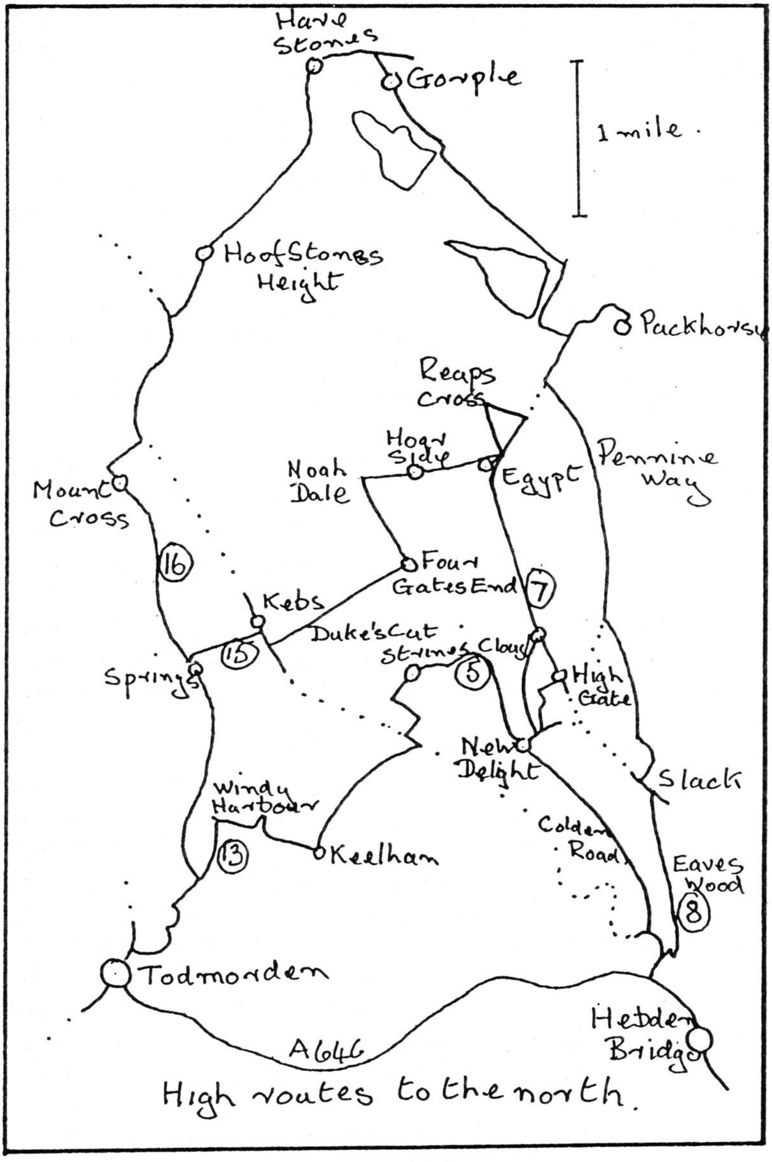

High routes to the north.

staying at one of the many bed and breakfast places, you can look up your nearest place in the index and you are en route to an interconnection point. You may even find that your own house is in the index. The walks are graded by height. The lower walks just get out of the valley bottom and meander along the agricultural plane the lies above the valley. The middle walks go a little higher, getting to the edge of the moors. The high walks get right on the tops and away into wild moorland.

The walks are described in both directions, walks 1 to 8 are the reverse of walks 9 to 16. There may be slight alterations if the gradient is too severe or reverse directions might be difficult to follow. The sketch maps are an aid to choosing a walk rather than an accurate representation of the route.

The mileage given at the start of the walk is determined by measurement on the Ordnance Survey map. The actual mileage will be slightly longer to take into account hills and dales. The time taken for each walk will vary from person to person. This book is published in my seventieth year and now I walk at about two miles an hour. I often stop and study the landscape or something close to the path. Groups of people also walk at about this speed - the speed of the slowest. Years ago I would have legged it over the moors at four miles an hour!

The reader has great flexibility in choosing a walk to match his or her stamina and preferences. If you are not used to doing much walking it is best to start by just doing one of the lower walks and at the end, take a bus or train back to the start. You could start a long weekend walk with a high route from one town to the other, have a pleasant lunch at one of many good eating-places and take a more leisurely walk back to your starting point. If the lunch has been too good, you can always follow the Rochdale canal from one town to other keeping to the valley bottom. The half-hourly bus will take you from one to the other in fifteen minutes and the train will do it in six minutes. Access by train is easy from York, Leeds, Bradford, Halifax, Rochdale, Manchester, Accrington, Blackburn, Preston and Blackpool. Both towns have car parks at the railway station which are free to rail users, although there is usually more room in the

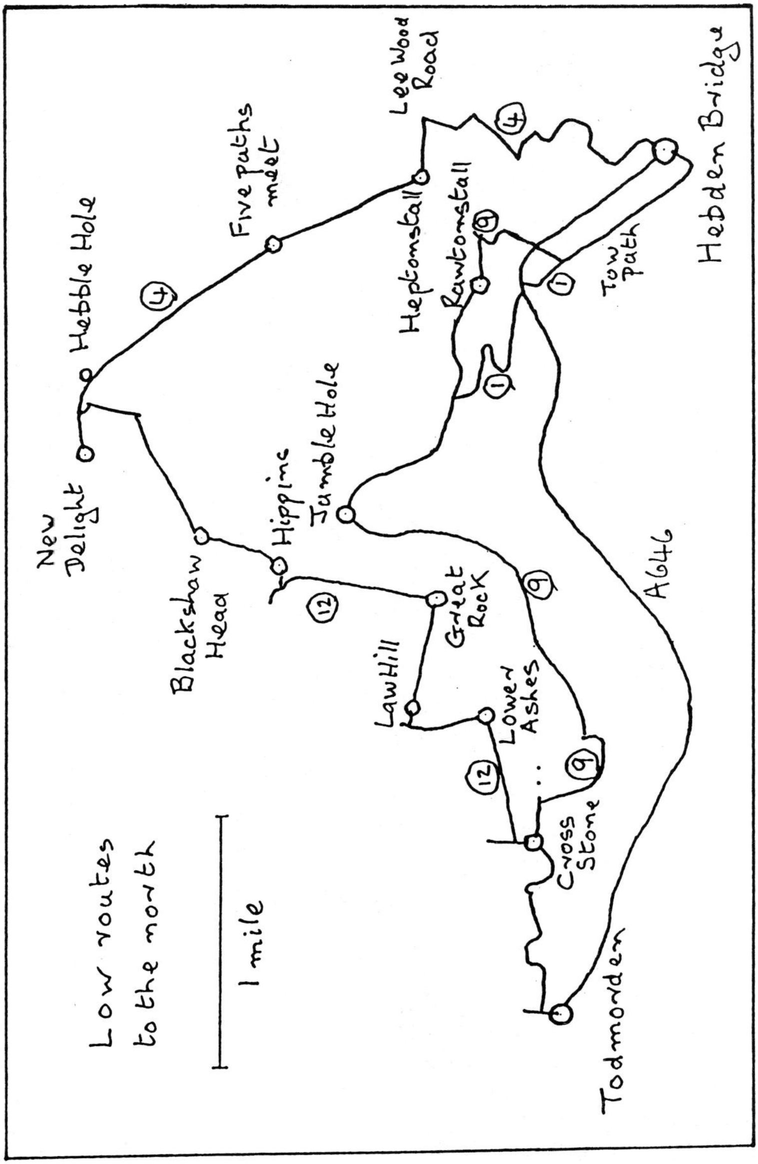
Low routes to the north
1 mile
Todmorden
Cross Stone
Lower Ashes
Law Hill
Great Rock
Blackshaw Head
New Delight
Hippins
Jumble Hole
Hebble Hole
Five paths meet
Heptonstall
Rawtonstall
Lee Wood Road
Hebden Bridge
Tow path
A646
4
9
12
1

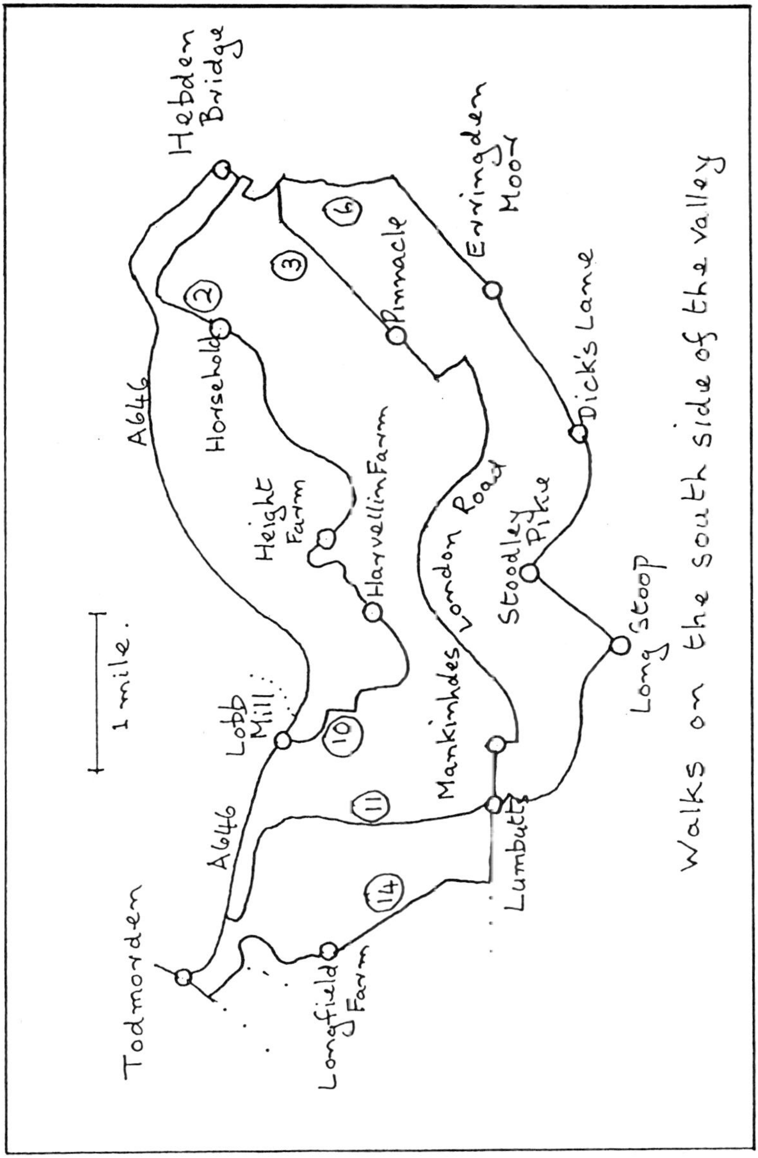

Walks on the south side of the valley

Todmorden station car park.

Outside rush hours both buses and trains between Todmorden and Hebden Bridge leave every thirty minutes. At the time of writing trains left Todmorden for Hebden Bridge at nineteen and fifty two minutes past the hour. They left Hebden Bridge for Todmorden at twenty-two and fifty two minutes past the hour. Local buses run to the north of Hebden Bridge to Heptonstall, Slack, New Delight and Blackshaw Head. Local buses run to the south of Todmorden to Lumbutts, Mankinholes and Harvelin Park. Lobb Mill is severd by buses from both towns. Travel information can be obtained from Metro, telephone 0113 245 7676.

Good footware is essential. In winter expect ice and snow. At any other time expect mud! Take note of the weather forecast and choose a route with the wind behind you. Tell someone what route you are taking and if you have a mobile phone put it in your rucksack. If you intend to walk over open moorland, take a compass with you and know how to use it. The South Pennine Leisure Map, scale 1:25,000, produced by the Ordnance Survey, covers all the routes in this book. It is worth getting the latest copy because rights of way and permissive paths do change. All routes in this book were walked between April and June 1999 and their accuracy has been checked against the definitive maps held by Calderdale Council. These were correct at the time of writing but there will be floods, landslides and diversions, which change routes in the future.

Many of the walks mention local pubs where you can get a meal and refreshment. These might not be to everyone's taste but they are part of our heritage on the tops. They were the equivalent of motorway service stations from the sixteenth century. You will find most hill side pubs open at lunchtimes at the weekend and on bank holidays, but many are closed mid week, particularly in the winter. If you are planning a walk and would like to stop at one of the old packhorse inns, it is as well to give them a ring the night before to check that they will be open. Many will open specially for walking parties if they have notice. Telephone numbers are listed on page 91.

Walk No. 1

Hebden Bridge to Todmorden via Stubbingg Wharf, Knott Wood, Jumble Hole, Eastwood, Ingham Clough, Cross Stone or Rodwell End and Lobb Mill.

Distance: 5.5 miles. Walking time: 2-3 hours. A low route.

From Hebden Bridge Tourist Information Centre cross Bridge Gate and New Road to go down Holme Street past the Post Office and Hebden Bridge Little Theatre to reach the canal towpath. Go right, past Blackpit Lock and Hebble End, under the bridge and past the two locks at Stubbings, under the next bridge to the pub at Stubbing Wharf. Leave the towpath here to rejoin the road. Cross the River Calder and the main Halifax Road, going left past Savile Road to take the next right up Oakville Road.

You are getting away from the traffic here and soon run out of footpath to follow Oakville Road. Once you are up to the level of the railway you have views across the valley to Callis Wood. Passing the cottages at Oakville **take the right track where the roads divide**, just past the red post-box. This is Turret Hall Road, a public bridleway. The track begins to wind through Knott Wood, full of bluebells in spring. Do not take the track to Wood Farm but **bear left with the cottages on your right**. A gap in the trees here gives you a good view back across the valley to Horsehold.

You soon pass a clearing in the wood, which is a workplace for making willow hurdles and logs for general use. You can follow the track to the top but it is a little more interesting to **take the public footpath on the left at the next corner**. This is the Pennine Way coming up! We are now high above Sandbed on the north side of the valley. **Where the path divides and the Pennine Way goes down to the left, we take the smaller path to the right**. This path is rather overgrown and could have done with a bit of maintenance last time I walked it. The hillside here is covered in wild flowers in spring. Keep following the wall on your right, and you soon hear the sound of water in Dole Clough. **At this point the path turns uphill past an old cottage dated 1764, to rejoin Winters Lane**. Go left with good views of Stoodley Pike on your left.

At the next junction go left past Long Hey Top and take the field path on the left immediately after Long Hey Top. Follow the power lines to the next farm. At last we have a bit of downhill all the way to the bridge at Jumble Hole Clough. **Keep to the right of the next farm and follow the green lane**. Look out for rabbits on your left! **The lane emerges onto the farm track to Dove Scout Farm. Follow the wall on the right behind the farm**. The track is now above Jumble Hole Clough that we have to cross and climb to a slightly higher level on the other side. Power lines indicate the general direction.

Various paths diverge on the way down to the bridge, so let the sound of water guide you down. There is a lovely old slab bridge across the clough. The flow and fall of water in this clough is so great that it once supplied several water-powered mills. **Once over the bridge we climb out of the valley bottom crossing two paths, at different levels, which run parallel to the stream. Once over the second path, the climb goes left and becomes steeper**, passing through heather, bracken and bilberries. The last bit is quite a pull up around the back of Roundfield Farm, which is down on your left. If the dogs spot you, they will do their job and bark like mad! **There is a stone stile before a final wooden stile to take you onto the downhill track to Roundfield Farm**. You are out of the valley now ready for some steady downhill walking.

When the track turns sharp left to Roundfield Farm, **continue downhill in the general direction of Stoodley Pike and then follow the track around to the right towards the next house at Hipperholm**. Avoid the grassy track that goes straight down to the valley bottom at Sandbed. **Continue along passing Hipperholm, Lane House Farm and Upper House Barn**. You may hear the screech of peacocks up on your right along this stretch. The tower of Cross Stone Church is ahead as you approach a T-junction. **At the junction you join Eastwood Lane, go downhill about ten paces, to the stone stile on your right. Follow an old causeway path, often buried, across five fields to a row of cottages at Chapel Houses. The right of way passes behind these houses, which you should keep on your left, until you reach the steps down in the corner of the last field to join a rather wet green lane. This leads down to the next house, Mount Pleasant. Just after Mount Pleasant cross the farm road and follow the green lane ahead.**

You can see how Mount Pleasant acquired its name; there could be nothing more pleasant than this green track which has been little used for a number of years. **Follow it straight ahead**, ignoring the left turn to Pex Tenements, towards the line of trees in Ingham Clough. The sound of water increases as various field drains join the stream beside the path until it becomes a veritable torrent, particularly after rain. Bluebells line the banks in spring as you **wend your way down to the footbridge across Ingham Clough. Once over the bridge the path follows the post and wire fence to the left, as far as a large beech tree. Then it the turns uphill to follow the wall to the top corner of the field.**

These fields have been extensively grazed by a herd of Welsh Black cattle that have lived on this land for thirty-five years to my knowledge. The farmhouse burnt down in the 1970s and the land has had little agricultural input apart from some late mowing since that time. In June the fields-free from cattle-are covered in wild flowers. The cattle themselves are very placid, and it would not be unusual to find cows, bulls and calves all intermixed. If they are in the way, or appear too interested in you, walk on while telling them in a low "mooing" voice telling them they are "good uns". At this, they will turn away and resume chewing the cud!

Follow the wall on the left across four fields to a little wooden gate on Matthew Lane. At this point there are alternative endings. So it is time to choose. The first alternative is definitly the more attractive but the second has advantages if you intend to return to Hebden Bridge on the south side of the valley without going into Todmorden, or if you fancy a pub lunch at the Rose and Crown.

FIRST ALTERNATIVE ENDING: **Follow the lane to the left for about sixty-five paces and then take the path on your right**, which drops down to a stream. It can be wet here. The path is fairly narrow, sometimes lined with rose-bay willow-herb and brambles and sometimes with oak and beech. Note the little white Clough Cottage down on your left. This only has a footpath to it - there is no road access. The path gradually climbs. Ignore the gate on the left and climb until Todmorden comes into view, **then continue on to the old farm at Bean Hole Head where you join Cross Stone Road. Going left, you pass the rather colourful gardens at Hollins Hall to arrive**

at the hamlet of Cross Stone. The building on your left is interesting. Note the inscription "Train up a child in the way he should go and when he is old he will not depart from it". This plaque was put there by Thomas Ashworth in 1805 when the top room was Cross Stone School. The bottom room was the jail and the right-hand end of the house was the home of the schoolmaster. The stocks are still in the wall backing onto the church. The church is now a private house and the old Bay Horse Inn has been renamed the Berghof Brandstatter and has been expanded to form a hotel and restaurant. I can remember the days when a pint of ale, served from a jug under a barrel tap, cost one shilling and five old pence!

Once past the Berghof we drop down Cross Stone hill. Todmorden unfolds before you. The legacies of the Fielden family stand out from the town. First the great spire of the Unitarian Church and then the Town Hall, both grade one listed buildings, provided by the Fieldens. Then there is Dobroyd Castle on the hillside opposite. Yet to come is Stansfield Hall. As you go round the fourth bend, just by a seat on the right, **take the footpath that goes off to the right**. Yellow broom lightens the path that soon goes between two rows of hawthorn trees on to The Mount. **Here we pass six houses and then go down the steps by the wall on the left**. This wall encircles Stansfield Hall, once a characteristic local hall. The Fieldens made additions to make it a much grander home. **At the bottom of the steps cross the road and go to the right past the playground to a path which crosses the railway by a footbridge on to Wellington Road. Take the first left, past Claremont Place and follow the road to the bottom passing the fire station, the ambulance station and the bus station in quick succession. Turn left at the bottom and go past the market to the end of the walk at the Town Hall**. A visit to the Tourist Information Centre is worthwhile.

SECOND ALTERNATIVE ENDING: **Follow the lane to the left**, and after the next corner, you are walking towards Stoodley Pike across the valley and towards the hamlet of Rodwell End, abandoned until the 1970s, it once had a manor house, a chapel, three farms and some workers' cottages. The census of 1841 revealed that it was a thriving place. Restoration is moving along slowly and the hamlet is gradually being brought back to life. The old farmhouse remains burnt out. The BBC Country File programme once gave a prize to the Ecological Building Society for its forward thinking in granting mortgages to people who wanted to restore these buildings. **Take the track, which turns right just before you reach the old chapel**, which you can recognise by its round top windows. **Go past the large barn on your right, which has a stone vaulted roof inside, and then bear left in the yard to follow the path down to the valley at Lobb Mill.**

The path zig-zags down the hillside. See how the road, the railway, the canal and the river compete for space in the valley bottom. Todmorden Town Hall can be spotted in the distance to your right. Soon you walk over the Horsefall railway tunnel, which was cut open, rebuilt and recovered in 1998, to reach the picnic site at the side of the main Halifax Road. **Cross over the road and walk to your right towards Todmorden and then take the first left, Haugh Road, where you can join the towpath for the last mile or so**. Lobb Mill Chandlers sell ropes, batteries and everything for the barge trade – but you can also buy ice cream.

Follow the towpath to the right. You are soon walking between the river and the canal. At the next bridge you see the fire-damaged Woodhouse Mill, built in 1832. It was once destined to be a textile museum but is up for sale at the time of writing. At this point you are about a mile from Todmorden town centre but less than 200 yards from the Rose and Crown, a diversion of about two hundred yards.

If you would like to take this diversion, climb the steps at the side of the bridge by the mill and follow the road to your right. The Rose and Crown is soon in view. Converted from three cottages, it is now a free house with good beer and food served every day from 12 to 2:30 p.m. If you get the taste and there is a good "crack" going on, there are buses outside the door to Todmorden and Hebden Bridge.

From the bridge on Woodhouse Road, the canal towpath forms a direct route to Todmorden. The next landmark is Oldroyd Lock. If it has been raining recently, water will be cascading down the overflows. Oldroyd Farm is on the knoll at the back of the lock. We are now into the industrial area of Todmorden. Warman International on your left produces huge pumps capable of emptying a coal mine or reservoir. The canal is home to ducks, geese and moorhens with nest sites on the far bank. After the next bridge you pass the new Baltimore Marina. Further on, there is an exit from the towpath into the Co-op supermarket car park. **Leave the canal at the next lock (Shop Lock)**. There are tea-rooms in the Craft Centre to your right behind the car park. **At the main road, turn left to Todmorden Town Centre**. The Tourist Information Centre and Bus station are in Burnley Road. To reach the railway station, go up the steps to the left of the White Hart, west of the Town Hall. Todmorden Market is worth a look round but it is closed on Mondays and Tuesdays.

Walk No. 2

Hebden Bridge to Todmorden. via Horsehold, Edge End Moor, Harvelin Park and Lobb Mill.

Distance: 5.5 miles. Walking time: 2-3 hours. A low route.

The starting point for walks from Hebden Bridge is the Tourist Information Centre at the junction of New Road and Bridge Gate, just by the traffic lights. Cross to the south side of New Road and go down Holme Street, past the Post Office and Hebden Bridge Little Theatre. Turn right on the canal bank and past Blackpit Lock No. 9. If you arrive in Hebden Bridge by train leave the station approach by the gate to Calder Holmes Park and walk through the park to cross the canal bridge just before Blackpit Lock, No 9.

Follow the towpath to the next bridge, which is backed by a tall chimney. **Leave the towpath at the bridge, cross the bridge and take New Road signed to Horsehold**. This is a bit of a pull out of the valley. It will get your heart and lungs up to speed – but at least you get the climbing over with at the start. This road is better going up than coming down! **At the next junction, continue to follow Horsehold Road straight ahead**. A welcome seat provided by Hepton Gala Committee in 1972 gives you good views across the valley. Below Heptonstall Church, on the skyline, is Eaves Wood. This extends to the left up the Colden Valley and just as it disappears round the corner you can see Lumb Bank, once the home of Ted Hughes, the late Poet Laureate. Lumb Bank is now part of the Arvon Foundation, which puts on courses for writers. The lower church at Mytholm caters for worshipers in the valley bottom. Incidentally 'myth' means the meeting of rivers and holme is flat land at the valley bottom.

Continue upwards until you come across a little gate on your right. This is about a hundred yards past the passing place and is signed as a public footpath. This is a worthwhile, very short diversion, to the seat on the top of Horsehold Crag. Straight across the valley lies a cluster of old houses at Rawtonstall. This is a very old settlemen, and the Doomsday Book records that there was a vinery there. On the rock in front of the seat, and slightly to the right, there is a circular hole, which is used to place an Easter Cross. The high ground to your left, on the opposite side of the valley, is Staups Moor, a mass of purple heather in August.

Return to the road and **continue upward where the tarmac soon gives way to old cobbles**. You are now out of the valley and into sheep country with Horsehold Farm on your left. Just before the **farm take the bridleway to the right signed to Horsehold Wood**, a mass of bluebells and wild garlic in May. Water trickles out of the wall-side crossing gritstone channels and then dropping quickly through the woods to the canal. Soon you see Edge End Farm on the hillside ahead. Our route will take us to the right of the farm. **When you reach a place where there are four gates, take the right hand one and go straight ahead**. Soon you hear a stream tumbling down on your right, which you will cross before long. Just after the stream comes into view, the paths divide. The left hand one is signed to Stoodley Pike but you **take the right hand one, go through the gate, over the bridge and climb to the road**. This is a beautiful part of the hillside.

The farm road is part of the Pennine Way. Cross it and go through the stile signed to Stoodley Pike and Edge End Moor. If it is not windy, about the only sounds you will hear are sheep and moorland birds, skylarks, curlews, and perhaps a cuckoo. **Continue to follow the wall on your right**, which is soon joined by tractor tracks coming down from Edge End Farm. Staups Moor is now prominent across the valley. Soon you see the ruins of Crutonstall Farm in the foreground. **When the tractor marks begin to drop towards the ruins you need to keep high, following the contours of the hill**. You are now below the edge of the moor and at the top of the agricultural plain. The path keeps to the high side of a wall far above the water treatment works at Sandbed below. **As you pass a second deserted farm, the path climbs slightly to follow a post and wire fence on your right**.

The monument on Stoodley Pike soon comes into view. **Through the next gate the path swings to the left and climbs around Higham**. Behind Higham you can see the next farm at Height Gate. Hawthorn trees give some softness to the landscape at this point. **The route behind Higham is marked with stones, which were painted white some time ago. The path drops down towards Height Gate. Just after the gate from**

the moor, the path turns sharp right. Do not follow it. Go straight on and then bear left towards the next deserted farm at Straight Hey (a grade two listed ruin). As soon as you reach a flat grassy track, notice the path below on your right which is coming up to meet you. This is the path you want, so double back down it. If you reach the walled path down to the bridge to Straight Hey, you have gone too far. The path is behind you!

The landmark ahead is the tower of Cross Stone Church on the opposite hillside. Your descent into Todmorden has started now, **so follow the valley down to a little white gate where you join the farm track coming down from Height Farm. The track follows the stream below on your left** passing through mixed woods of silver birch, holly, oak and sycamore. As the track zig-zags down the hill it is possible to cut off a corner but it is safer to keep to the track. **At the second bend, take the path down to the stream, signed public bridleway to Stoodley. Cross the stepping stones and go through the gate**. The track is very rough here and could do with some infill but you soon reach a good surface at Stock Hey. **The route for the next mile is straight ahead to Harvelin Park, passing Middle Stoodley and Higher Stoodley**, with its lovely walled garden, on the way. Ahead right, the television repeater mast is an obvious landmark. Just below it is Shaw Farm with a wall leading away from it to the right. You will soon be following a path by the side of it. **Pass Fielden House and the newer houses at Harvelin Park**. There is an hourly bus service to Todmorden from here if you need it.

At the end of Lee Bottom Road follow the road around to the right, take the next left, New Road, and you soon reach Shaw Farm on your right. The electric gates look a bit intimidating but you are on a public footpath, and the gates will open and close for you at the push of a button. Cross the yard to a chorus of barking dogs, which fortunately are chained, to the right hand gate at the far end of the yard. The yard doubles as a helicopter landing pad so, if you see one coming, do the sensible thing and wait until it has landed and the rotors have stopped! **Now follow the old causeway stones between the wall and the hawthorn trees**. You may come across an electric fence, which you can open and close using the orange insulated handles. **At the end of the causeway, pass through two gates to a**

path that drops down to the valley bottom at Lobb Mill. The canal is soon in view. Before you reach it, you join Haugh Road that comes up to the house and newly restored barn at Haugh. At this point you have a good view of the railway viaduct to the left and the newly reconstructed tunnel to the right. Note the path below this tunnel, which is part of the low route from Todmorden to Hebden Bridge on the north side of the valley.

Walk down to the canal at Lobb Mill. The mill itself was demolished in the 1930s. The Chandlers at Lobb Mill do sell ice cream. If your plan is to walk back to Hebden Bridge, you need not continue to Todmorden. You can cross the main Halifax Road and walk to your right to the picnic site where you pick up the path which you have previously noted. The route back is described on page 55. If your plan is to walk to Todmorden, or have a pub lunch, **your route is along the tow-path to the west**. You are soon walking between the river and the canal. At the next bridge you see the fire-damaged Woodhouse Mill, built in 1832. It was once destined to be a textile museum but was up for sale at the time of writing. At this point you are about a mile from Todmorden town centre but less than 200 yards from the Rose and Crown, a diversion of about two hundred yards.

If you would like to take this diversion, **climb the steps at the side of the bridge by the mill and follow the road to your right**. The Rose and Crown is soon in view. Converted from three cottages, it is now a free house with good beer and food served every day from 12 to 2:30 pm. If you get the taste and there is a good "crack" going on, there are buses outside the door to Todmorden and Hebden Bridge.

From the bridge on Woodhouse Road, the canal tow-path forms a direct route to Todmorden. The next landmark is Oldroyd Lock. If it has been raining recently, water will be cascading down the overflows. Oldroyd Farm is on the knoll at the back of the lock. You are now into the industrial area of Todmorden. Warman International on your left produces huge pumps capable of emptying a coal mine or reservoir. The canal is home to ducks, geese and moorhens with nest sites on the far bank. After the next bridge you pass the new Baltimore Marina. Further on, there is an exit from the towpath into the Co-op supermarket car park. **Leave the canal at the next lock (Shop Lock)**. There is a tea-room in the craft centre to your right behind the car park. **At the main road, turn left to Todmorden Town Centre**. The Tourist Information Centre and Bus station are in Burnley Road. To reach the railway station, go up the steps to the left of the White Hart, west of the Town Hall. Todmorden Market is worth a look round but it is closed on Mondays and Tuesdays.

Walk No. 3

Hebden Bridge to Todmorden via Palace House Road, Crow Wood, Pinnacle, London Road, Mankinholes, Lumbutts and Key Sike Lane.

Distance: 5.5 miles. Walking time: 2-3 hours. A medium route.

There are two alternative routes to the starting point in Palace House Road. If you arrive by train, turn right as you come out of the booking office – almost everybody else will turn left. Go under the railway bridge and turn right into Palace House Road. You need to walk for about a quarter of a mile along here, aiming for the television mast. As the road begins to descend, take the first track to the left before the traffic lights. This is the start.

If you are starting from the Tourist Information Centre in Bridge Gate, cross to the south side of New Road and go down Holme Street, past the Post Office to cross the canal bridge. Once over the bridge go right and climb the steps to Shelf Road. Turn left, cross the railway bridge and you are in Palace House Road. Take the first track on the right and you are at the starting point.

From the starting point, walk up the lane for about one hundred yards then take the green lane on the right that climbs to a line of trees. This is the start of Crow Nest Wood. Just before the line of trees, an old wall goes up the hillside on the left through the wood. **The path follows the line of this wall**. The going is quite steep and care is needed. Towards the top, boulders are strewn amongst the bluebells. **At the top, take the steps to the stile, cross the track and take the signed path to Pinnacle Lane**.

This path follows the wall across five fields, and by the time you reach the third field, most of the climbing is over. It is time to give yourself a rest and take note of the panoramic view behind you. Looking from right to left, the television mast is in the foreground and in the distance are Old Town and Wadsworth. Hebden Bridge is in the valley, with the wooded Hebden Valley behind it. On the hill opposite is Heptonstall Church, and the Colden Valley is below it, with Ted Hughes' old house, Lumb Bank, below the houses at Slack. Further to the left is the hamlet of Rawtonstall, then Calder Valley and on the skyline to the left, Staups Moor.

Continue to follow the wall. By the time you reach the fourth field, the peace monument on Stoodley Pike dominates the skyline. Our route will follow the hillside to the right of the monument. **At the fifth field, follow the farm track towards Stoodley Pike. At the road, follow the sign to Stoodley Pike down Pinnacle Lane**. The farm across the fields on the left is Erringden Grange. Note how sycamore trees are planted in the corner of the field to provide shelter. **You soon pass Pinnacle Farm on the right**. A good watchdog may announce your presence, but it is docile enough.

Beyond Pinnacle Farm the track becomes a green road and eventually rather a wet green road until you pass the wood coming up from the right. Follow the track around an S-bend to the next gate. The path now follows the wall on the left across two fields, towards Stoodley Pike, to a farm lane. At this lane, turn left and follow it for about a quarter of a mile to the next junction where you turn right towards Swillington.

Passing Swillington, go through the gate and begin your descent to Todmorden. You soon cross the Pennine Way coming down from Stoodley Pike. The track is now called London Road, which you follow for just over two miles to Mankinholes. Although the track is rough underfoot, the views to the right are a real joy. When I walked this route in May the cuckoos were sounding off in the valley below. Once past the Pennine Way, you can catch a glimpse of Todmorden Town Hall in the distance – before you lose too much height. About half way along London Road you pass a path coming up from Harvelin Park on the right, straight up to the Pike on the left.

London Road leaves Langfield Common at a gate before Mankinholes. When you reach Mankinholes, turn right and walk through this pretty village for about two hundred yards to a path on the left, which is just after Mankinholes Youth Hostel. Cross the stile and follow the paved path across the field to the Top Brink Inn at Lumbutts. As you go, the tall steep roof of Lumbutts Chapel is on your left. The square tower of Lumbutts Mill, which once housed three water wheels, is ahead. **Pass in front of the Top Brink**, which normally opens at 7 p.m. On Saturdays it is also open from noon to

2:30pm and on Sundays and Bank Holidays it is open from noon to 10:30pm.

Once past the pub, make towards the old farmyard to the left of the cottages. At the end of the yard go through the little gate and follow the causeway stones as they switch wall sides, to a tall stile in the wall ahead. In the next field go half-right, uphill in the general direction of Whirlaw Stones on the far side of the valley. At the top of the field the view across to Cross Stone opens up and **the path begins to drop down to follow a post and wire fence** around the old landfill site at Folly. Note the ventilation shafts to let the methane out. **As you reach a cinder track, follow it downhill to join Woodhouse Road. Here you go right to the first corner. At the end of the fence on the left is a little used path that goes between two walls. Keep the house on your right and press ahead to a slab-bridge and stile into the next field. Here you go left to the next bridge and gate and then right to the next stile. At this point, maintain your height and make towards the new houses on the far side. There is a little gate just above the bottom house. Go right through this gate and it brings you out into Summerfield Road. You can take any of the paths or streets on your right to lead you down to a path along the high side of the canal. Follow the white railings to Key Sike Lane. Cross the canal bridge and turn left on to the towpath to Todmorden. You can leave the towpath at Shop Lock, No.18, for the tea room at the Craft Centre. At the main road go left to the Town Hall**. The Tourist Information Centre is at 15, Burnley Road. If you like, you can follow the towpath to Todmorden Lock, No.19. As you go under Rochdale Road, note the grooves in the stone worn deep by ropes from horse-drawn barges. Once on Rochdale Road go left to the Town Hall, bus and railway stations.

Walk No. 4

Hebden Bridge to Todmorden via Heptonstall, Hebble Hole, Blackshaw Head, Great Rock, and Cross Stone.

Distance: 7.5 miles. Walking time: 4 hours. A medium route.

No book on walks between Hebden Bridge and Todmorden could possibly omit Heptonstall, an old hilltop village in a fine defensive position surrounded on three sides by steeply sloping land to a river at the bottom. Heptonstall is well worth exploring and you can buy a guide-book to the village. Hebden Bridge grew around the old pack horse bridge across the River Hebden. The direct route from the old bridge to Heptonstall is up The Buttress, a very steep, cobbled road described by Thomas Twinning in the eighteenth century as almost vertical! The route up The Buttress is well signed from the bridge and you can walk it if you like, but residents of Heptonstall say that by far the best way up is by bus. There are two buses per hour, a double decker and a mini bus, but their departure times from Hebden Bridge are usually close together.

My favourite route goes up in three stages, with plenty of time to get your breath back in between. **Starting from the Tourist Information Centre, walk along Bridge Gate** (which means the way to the bridge) **to the old bridge, cross it and turn right immediately after the Hole in the Wall pub. Continue along Hangingroyd Lane to the end, where you go right then left crossing the river again and following the road round into Victoria Road**. The view along Victoria Road is worth studying. The steepness of the hillside to Heptonstall is obvious, the village is over the skyline. Across the valley the houses at Hollins are dotted among the trees. You will be walking among them in a few minutes. **At the end of Victoria Road go right and then left to an old packhorse bridge**.

Cross the bridge and go straight ahead past the cricket ground and archery field. Soon you get a taste of climbing this hillside up a cobbled path, with steps and a handrail. **When the handrail ceases, turn right along the causeway and follow the wall** along a path that is full of wild flowers in summer. You go through some rhododendron bushes, past No.14 **and take the path ahead on the same level. You have hardly**

started before there is a choice of paths. It does not matter which one you take, they both climb through the woods to a track on the second level up.

On reaching the track, turn right. At the next junction take the left fork, signed to Hardcastle Crags and the Scout Hostel. Just as you hit the tarmac, there is a little-used path on the left that climbs through the woods again. This is a useful short cut but if you miss it, follow the tarmac road until you meet the Calderdale Way crossing it. Then turn left up the Calderdale Way. The short cut comes out onto the Calderdale Way higher up. Walk up the track and cross Lee Wood Road to North Well Lane, which is signed as a bridleway to Heptonstall. At the next junction, take the right track past three houses to emerge in front of Northfield Terrace. If you happen to walk this path in February, you will be rewarded with the sight of snowdrops.

Follow the road, Northgate, to the left. On your left is the octagonal Methodist Chapel built in 1764. On your right, notice the old lintel dated 1578 carrying the initials of John Bentley. Our way ahead will go under this lintel but for the moment it is worth a walk a little further on to the centre of the village. Opposite No.3 Wadsworth view, the old door has a carved panel above it with the initials of Henry Foster and his wife Elizabeth, dated 1736. You emerge onto Towngate next to the Cross Inn. Heptonstall Post Office, just downhill, sells a guide to the village. You could spend hours here looking at all the historical buildings. **When you are ready to leave, return to Northgate and go under the old lintel dated 1578. Note the plaque on the end of Whitehall Farm, continue across Whitehall Fold to a stile leading to a path that runs behind the houses and past the school, to cross the road above the village.**

Take the path on the left signed to Lumb Bank, Ted Hughes' old house. The path crosses a field that is a mass of buttercups in June. **Beyond the next stile you pass the house with the tall chimney, cross the lane and continue along the side of two fields to Field Farm. Walk along the line of conifers behind it to the next little gate. The path follows the wall to a star junction of five paths. Follow the Calderdale Way signs on the second path on the right along the causeways and power lines, past the next house. Look out for a left turn before the next gate.**

Weavers Square, Heptonstall. Always a delight at any time of the year. In summer the containers of plants catch the eye.

The opposite hillside is sprouting with self-seeded trees. **A hundred yards downhill your route bears right, crossing the fields towards the top of Foster Wood. Cross into the wood and go right down to the river at Hebble Hole**. The grassy patch and bilberry-covered banks make a pleasant to stop for Pennine Way walkers who also have to cross the old bridge. **Once over the bridge there is a steep scramble to Colden Road, an old bridleway. Go right here, pass the site of Hudson Mill**, once one of many water-powered mills in this valley. Note the empty millpond. **Some sixty paces beyond the entrance to the mill there is a left turn. Our route takes this turn** but it is worth mentioning that the New Delight is 300 yards along Colden Road, and, at the time of writing, is open all day every day. **Take the left turn up to Shaw Bottom and then follow the rough track up the hill**. It is fairly steep going, but a rest will give you a chance to look back over the Colden Valley from Heptonstall to Egypt. **About 250 yards up the track, look out for a small gate on the right. This leads to a path that crosses seven fields diagonally to emerge on Badger Lane at Blackshaw Head.**

At Badger Lane there is another good pub, the Shoulder of Mutton, about 150 yards to your right. At the time of writing, Serena and Allan will welcome you for lunch on Friday to Sunday from noon. If you go there, note the milestone to London, 206 miles, at the corner of the chapel.

Our route crosses Badger Lane and takes the farm track. As the track turns into the yard, follow the causeways to the right. You can see Staups Moor ahead, which is a mass of purple heather in August. Listen for moorland birds – snipe, curlew, peewits and skylarks abound round here. **Keep to the left of the next farm and follow the causeways again**, now built over a drain.

After Apple Tree Farm the path follows a post and wire fence to an old barn above Hippins Farm. Continue on to Hippins Farm and note its date stone – 1656. This is the era when timber frame buildings were being replaced with stone buildings and many of the farms in this area date from that time. Beyond the farm you reach Hippins Bridge. Hippins is an old Yorkshire name for stepping-stones. The bridge replaced the hippins in 1883. Note the new wall to your left. This wall was built in 1999 following heavy rains that washed the road into the clough. **Cross Hippins Bridge and take the stile on the right to climb out of the valley. Once out, the route goes to a tall wooden stile onto an old bridleway. The path continues along the edge of Staups Moor and crosses a goit that feeds Staups Dam**, once the power source for Eastwood Mill.

As you reach the stile at the end of the moor, it is worth having a look around. Hebden Bridge is to your left, Stoodley Pike ahead and now it is downhill all the way to Todmorden. You can soon see Staups Reservoir on the left with the new buildings that are part of the proposed fish farm. At the end of the lane, Great Rock is worth a climb to see the curve of the Calder Valley from Hebden Bridge to the tower of Cross Stone Church, another landmark on our way ahead. This is a great vantage point.

Turn right up Eastwood Road to the next junction, Crossley New Road, signed to Todmorden. Turn down the hill for a few yards and pick up the Calderdale Way that follows a green road. The walls here were rebuilt as part of the Community Programme when many unemployed people gained the skills of dry-stone walling. **Just after the second stile follow the Calderdale Way down to the left, passing three farms to Law Hill. Skirt above the first farm, Higher Birks, and drop down to the clough, then follow the path to Butts Lane**, which is virtually impassable but is easily crossed.

From Butts Lane the path passes Killup Farm and Cottage, crosses a green lane and climbs to the top of Law Hill, another good view point. From Stoodley Pike (going clockwise) you see Langfield Edge, across the valley, Rough Hill, Limers Gate and Flowerscar, with Whirlaw Rocks on this side. In the foreground is Cross Stone Church.

At the next stile you leave the Calderdale Way and go downhill to join the farm track past Broad Ing Top. Follow it down to Higher Ashes, and go left. Note the old single story cottage dated 1714, now used as a stable. **At the next farm, Lower Ashes, dated 1759, turn right and follow the grass track, keeping the house on your left. This leads to a stile and a path across four fields**. These are used for silage and grazing sheep, so keep close to the left wall. You come out onto Hey Head Lane, opposite Todmorden Golf Course. Go down the road to the junction with Cross Stone Road. The church is being converted to a private house.

As you drop down Cross Stone Hill, Todmorden unfolds before you. The legacies of the Fielden family stand out from the town, first the great spire of the Unitarian Church and then the Town Hall, both grade one listed buildings provided by the Fieldens. Then there is Dobroyd Castle on the hillside opposite. Yet to come is Stansfield Hall. **As you go round the fourth bend, just by a seat on the right, take the footpath that goes off to the right**. Yellow broom lightens the path that soon goes between two rows of hawthorn trees on to The Mount. Here you pass six houses and then go down the steps by the wall on the left. This wall encircles Stansfield Hall, once a characteristic local hall onto which the Fieldens built additions to make it a much grander home.

At the bottom of the steps, cross the road and go to the right past the playground to a path which crosses the railway by a footbridge on to Wellington Road. Take the first left, past Claremont Place and follow the road to the bottom passing the fire station, the ambulance station and the bus station in quick succession. Turn left at the bottom and go past the market to the end of the walk at the Town Hall. A visit to the Tourist Information Centre is worthwhile.

Walk No. 5

Hebden Bridge to Todmorden via Colden Clough, Jack Bridge, Strines Clough, Higher Back Lane, Harleywood Gate, Back of Behind, Keelham, Windy Harbour and Hole Bottom.

Distance: 7.5 miles. Walking time: 3-4 hours. A medium route.

From Hebden Bridge Tourist Information Centre cross Bridge Gate and New Road to go down Holme Street past the Post Office and Hebden Bridge Little Theatre to reach the canal towpath. Go right past Blackpit Lock and Hebble End, under the bridge and past two locks at Stubbings. Look out for a path on your right. It is about twenty paces after milestone No. 6. Pass the cottage at Stubbing Square on your left, cross the footbridge over the River Calder and follow Colden Water upstream to the main road. This is the last time that you will be on a level with Colden Water for a couple of miles.

Cross the main road to Church Lane. Once past the church, bear left uphill to the next corner where you pick up the bridleway to Jack Bridge. Old causeway stones soon appear as the tarmac runs out. It appears that this was originally a double causeway for carts and the route has been widened on the downhill side. The left causeway is often under the leaf mould from the trees. Soon you meet the first of twelve take-offs, designed to turn surplus water off the track to prevent it being washed away. They are beautifully made with nicely jointed gritstone.

Once past three houses you can see Ted Hughes' old house at Lumb Bank across the valley. **About three hundred yards, after the three houses, take the left track uphill**. The chimneys in the wood were for mills where water-power had been replaced by steam engines. Coal would have to be carted from Hebden Bridge and eventually these mills became uneconomic. There was even a silk mill in this valley.

You climb more steeply now, the wooded banks gradually opening up and the plants changing to bracken, heather and bilberry. As the path begins to level out, you are high enough to see the line of cottages at Colden Row on your right. **You cross**

the Pennine Way coming down from Pry Hill and down to the old bridge at Hebble Hole Bridge. Soon the New Delight is seen ahead.

Just after the New Delight take the track on the left before you cross Jack Bridge. You are still following Colden Water upstream behind a line of hawthorn and beech trees. At the end of the trees the stream passes under the delightful little Strines Bridge. You start climbing now, passing Strines, with its assorted windows, and Higher Strines. Note the magnificent house on your left with seven windows on the first floor. This is Field Head Farm that you will pass shortly.

About sixty paces beyond the entrance to Field Head farmyard, take the track to the left and go through the gate onto the bridleway. To the left you have good views down Colden Valley and Heptonstall Church is once again a landmark. The bridleway ahead has been restored. The sounds of moorland birds will be ringing in your ears if you walk this way in spring or early summer. At the next gate you can see the house called Strines Clough, with its clock tower over the stables. **At Strines Clough go right into the yard and take the gate on the left**. This is a continuation of the bridleway, which you can follow to Higher Back Lane. At this point, turn left to avoid the final section of the bridleway, which is so boggy a horse can sink up to its belly!

Take the second turning on the right off Higher Back Lane to come out onto the main road opposite Lower Moss Hall. Turn left and cross the road to face oncoming traffic. Drivers tend to drive along this stretch at high speed. Fortunately you only have about 150 yards to travel before you **turn off to the right down the drive to Harleywood Gate**. This is a private house, with a red telephone box in the garden, **but there is a footpath passing to the right of the house. Keep all buildings on your left and find the stile to a green road, which is walled off after 100 yards. At this point you make a left turn and aim for a breached reservoir across the valley**. You are now crossing a rather neglected area. The money in farming has gone. The stiles on this section need replacing, some are fenced off while others are rotten. **You cross two short fields, and then in the final field before the stream, aim for the ruined house called Copley Holme. Cross an old slab bridge**

Lumb Bank, Colden Valley. Once the home of Ted Hughes, the late poet laureate, and his wife Sylvia Plath, it now belongs to The Arvon Foundation and is a centre to encourage creative writing.

with an iron handrail and climb the steps carefully.

The reservoir to your left was used to store water in times of plenty, the water being released in times of shortage to power the five mills in Jumble Hole Clough downstream. The waterman also controlled the goit to Staups Dam, behind Great Rock, which in turn powered the mill at Eastwood. No wonder a house had to be built in such an important place!

Once up the steps you can either go to the old house and follow a bridleway beyond to the right, or you **can cut diagonally across the field to the right to the far corner. There is a stile in the corner that connects to a route that passes the next house, Back of Behind, passing it to the left of the house. Here you join a cinder track that takes you up to Eastwood Road. Cross the road, following the signed track to Cross Stone. This has a limestone surface and is called Keelham Lane. As the track turns into Keelham Farm, take the stile on the right and follow the wall, through the next stile and past an old quarry to join Broad Lane opposite Hall Stones Green Farm. Follow the road downhill and pass the two houses at Lower Winsley to pick up the bridleway towards Whirlaw at the next corner**.

Todmorden can be seen in the distance. Notice the farm half left with a green roofed building. This is Greenhurst Hey and you will be passing it shortly. **The track drops down and crosses a small stream**. As you rise on the other side, note the power lines coming down from Windy Harbour on your right to Greenhurst Hey on your left. Todmorden is clearly in view now. **Take the stile and follow the power lines downhill to Greenhurst Hey**. The meadows around this farm are full of wild flowers. The track is a bit of a knee-shaker going downhill. Follow it through the cobbled yard to the field below the house.

Stoodley Pike stands out again and Todmorden Golf Course, with its Bronze Age circle on the sixth fairway, lies below it on this side of the valley. Soon you hear the sound of water as you pass Latchford Cottage to **cross the Calderdale Way to take the link path all the way down to Todmorden**. The track twists and turns, never far away from the stream and goes past some beautiful homes, old and new, in Hole Bottom Road.

Todmorden is soon in sight. At the Fountain Inn turn right down Victoria Road. Once under the railway bridge,

take the first left along Railway Street. After you pass Hawthorn Place cross Wellington Road into Stansfield Road and go down it past the fire, ambulance and bus stations to reach Burnley Road. Go left here, past Todmorden Market to the Town Hall. The Tourist Information Centre is just across the road at 15, Burnley Road.

Walk No. 6

Hebden Bridge to Todmorden via Old Chamber, Erringden Moor, Dick's Lane, Stoodley Pike, Lumbutts and Longfield.

Distance: 7 miles. Walking time: 3-4 hours. A high route.

There are two alternative starts to this walk, either from Hebden Bridge railway station or from the Tourist Information Centre.

FIRST ALTERNATIVE: From the railway station turn right as you leave the booking office – almost everybody else will be going left. Drop down to the lane and go under the railway bridge and past the end of Palace House Road towards the tree-lined lane. Just behind the houses on your right, follow a track with a concrete surface up along the bottom of Crow Nest Wood until the path levels out at an X-junction. Take the top left path and continue to follow the wall along the bottom edge of the wood to the next X-junction. Here you double back left uphill to the clear sky beyond the wood.

SECOND ALTERNATIVE: From the Tourist Information Centre cross New Road to the south side and go down Holme Street past the Post Office and Hebden Bridge Little Theatre. Cross the canal bridge and turn right, following the steps up to Shelf Road where you turn left. Cross the railway bridge into Palace House Road and take the first track on your right. This has various surfaces but continue to the bottom of Crow Nest Wood where you meet the track coming up from the railway station. This is an X-junction. Take the top left path up through the wood to the clear sky beyond.

At the top of Crow Nest Wood take the stile with sheep netting across it and follow the causeway stones across three fields where the path turns right up to the farm. A yellow diamond marker shows the way. Go past the sheep pens and cross the lane to the next stile. In the first field you go diagonally left to a stile above two gates and then follow the

wall to rejoin the farm lane near the power lines. Go through the farmyard and follow the gated track climbing steadily past two houses. There are good views of the Calder Valley from Mytholmroyd as far as the Wainhouse Tower in Halifax.

Take the signed footpath on the right before you reach the third house. This follows an old sunken path to a stile on the edge of Erringden Moor. The way-marking sign points straight across the moor – but the path underfoot soon disappears. Crossing the moor can be exhilarating in good weather. The bottom edge of the moor is fairly wet and you have to pick your way carefully. Once you are about two hundred yards onto the moor you should be able to see the power lines running along the opposite edge and Stoodley Pike should be visible. **Your route is slightly to the left of Stoodley Pike going towards the power lines before they dip to the right, about 210 degrees on the compass**. If you are crossing in spring or summer the moorland birds will be in full cry, distracting you from their nest sites.

As you **cross the moor** to Dick's Lane, Rake Head Farm is a landmark on the right skyline. The wall between you and Rake Head runs up the to the highest point of the moor at Dick's Lane, before the power lines start to dip to the right. **Dick's Lane is a broad grass track**, occasionally used by tractors. There is a sheep fence half way along and **then you pass a scots pine plantation on your left. At the far end, Dick's Lane opens out into a field. Follow the wall on your right past the Pennine Way stile to a stone stile onto Langfield Common**. Stoodley Pike is straight ahead. The view to your right shows the Cross Stone hillside across the valley, topped by Staups Moor, purple with heather in August. In the foreground below is Edge End Moor.

As the well-worn Pennine Way rises to the Pike, there is an old stone trough on the left, inscribed "Public slakin trough". It is only a few feet below the top of the moor but it never runs dry. Green algae has appeared in it lately so I have stopped using it for slaking!

There are thirty-nine steps in a dark circular staircase inside the monument on Stoodley Pike to reach the balcony. Count them as you go and hope that you do not meet any sheep coming down! **From Stoodley Pike you follow the Pennine Way south for about twenty minutes' walk** whereupon you see a standing stone, known as Long Stoop, marking the summit of the causeway coming up from Lumbutts. There is a seat, just below Long Stoop on the right. This is in a splendid position and was erected in memory of Arthur Archer, one time warden of Mankinholes Youth Hostel. **At Long Stoop you turn right and walk down the causeway to Lumbutts.**

Notice how well the stones have been fitted together. These causeways used to be the old highways. Records in Calderdale Archives show the accounts of the Langfield surveyors, between 1725 and 1735, when most of these causeways were built. I have an illustrated talk on these old highways, which can be shown to interested parties.

The dams behind Lumbutts Mill once powered three water wheels in the square tower to the right of them. **Go through the gate at the bottom of the causeway and continue down the green lane to emerge opposite Lumbutts Chapel. Turn left down into the village.** The Top Brink is open at lunchtimes on weekends and bank holidays but there is no lunchtime opening on weekdays. The sound of water overflowing from Lee Dam is never far from your ears. Most of the mill has been demolished but new extensions form Lumbutts Activity Centre, now used for residential training weekends and other activities.

Follow Lumbutts Road uphill past the top of Causeway Wood Road and Causeway Wood West to the next house, which is dated 1598 above the door. Turn right just before this house following the Calderdale Way signs. Bear left through the farmyard and follow the green lane to a stile on your left. This is signed again. The footpath crosses six fields to Higher Longfield Farm. By the time you reach the third field, Todmorden is fully in view. You may be lucky enough to hear the sound of bells from the peel in the Unitarian Church.

The path goes to the left in front of Higher Longfield Farm. You do not need to follow the Calderdale Way if you do not want to. **There is a short cut following the farm track to the right, towards Dobroyd Castle on the opposite hillside ahead. Drop down to the houses at Longfield Terrace then turn right following the road downhill to Fielden Square and the Golden Lion. Todmorden Town Hall is a short distance along Rochdale Road to your right.**

Walk No. 7

Hebden Bridge to Todmorden via Colden Road, New Delight, Reaps Cross, Egypt, Stansfield Moor, Bride Stones and Meadow Bottom.

Distance: 10.5 miles. Walking time: 4-5 hours. A high route.

From Hebden Bridge Tourist Information Centre cross Bridge Gate and New Road to go down Holme Street past the Post Office and Hebden Bridge Little Theatre to reach the canal towpath. Go right past Blackpit Lock and Hebble End, under the bridge and past two locks at Stubbings. Look out for a path on your right. It is about twenty paces after milestone No. 6. Pass the cottage at Stubbing Square on your left, cross the footbridge over the River Calder and follow Colden Water upstream to the main road. This is the last time that you will be on a level with Colden Water for a couple of miles.

Cross the main road to Church Lane. Once past the church bear left, uphill to the next corner where you pick up the bridleway to Jack Bridge. Old causeway stones soon appear as the tarmac runs out. It appears that this was originally a double causeway for carts and the route has been widened on the downhill side. The left causeway is often under the leaf mould from the trees. Soon you meet the first of twelve take-offs, designed to take surface water off the track to prevent it being washed away. These are beautifully made with nicely jointed gritstone.

Once past three houses, you can see Ted Hughes' old house at Lumb Bank across the valley. **About three hundred yards after the three houses take the left track uphill**. The chimneys in the wood were for mills where water-power had been replaced by steam engines. Coal would have to be carted from Hebden Bridge and eventually these mills became uneconomic. There was even a silk mill in this valley.

You climb more steeply now, the wooded banks gradually opening up and the plants changing to bracken, heather and bilberry. As the path begins to level out, you are high enough to see the line of cottages at Colden Row on your right. **You cross the Pennine Way**, coming down from Pry Hill to the old bridge at Hebble Hole. Soon the New Delight is seen ahead.

Walk down past the New Delight and go up Smithy Lane, turning left just after Colden School. Follow the grassy track to the next farm. When you are about half way, note the pretty Strines Bridge in the field on the left. **Once through the farmyard, follow the road up to Edge Lane. Turn left, passing Longtail Cottage**. The trees in the valley around Land Farm and Salt Pie were planted in the 1970s. **Follow the track for about twenty minutes until you come to the gate on to Heptonstall Moor**. The farm on the left is called Egypt and you will pass it shortly, but you have an opportunity for an interesting diversion on Heptonstall Moor lasting 25 minutes. If you do not want to take it, ignore the next paragraph.

Follow the permissive bridleway towards Lower Gorple and note the power line posts. At the third post the bridleway goes left but you should follow the lines to the fifth post. Just to the west of this you will find an old causeway and a signpost marked to CLN 6 M (to Colne 6 miles). In fact the distance is 8 miles because this post is marked in old Lancashire miles which pre-date the statute of 1594 which defined the mile. The old Lancashire mile was one and a third statute miles. There are three other milestones, marked in old miles, in Todmorden. **Standing on the causeway and looking at the milestone, you will see the corner of a walled field about 200 yards away. Walk towards this corner and as you approach it you will see a standing stone just to the right of it. This is Reaps Cross**. It was made in three parts. The base and bottom part has stood for many years but the top portion was fastened with metal bands and broke off. It has been lying on the ground for many years. At the time of writing, there is a plan to repair it to mark the millennium. Hopefully it will have been done by the time you read this. **Return to the gate where you came onto the moor and turn right to pass behind Egypt**.

When you pass Egypt, the moor ahead is Stansfield Moor and the cluster of trees below it are around Hoar Side which you will pass in about 20 minutes. **About 300 yards after Egypt, pass to the left of a ruin to a stone stile. Follow the right wall to the bridge and follow the path to the left beyond it. There are occasional causeways on the way to Hoar Side. Pass below Hoar Side and take the track down to the ruined farm**

at Colden Water. The track climbs again after Colden Water and then it becomes a green lane. Follow this until you come to a walled lane down to the left leading to a bridge.

Once over the bridge and stile, the path keeps close to the left wall but is often a few yards from it to avoid wet patches. You are on the edge of Stansfield Moor. Follow the wall up to Four Gates End and turn right on to Dukes Cut. This track is called Dukes Cut after Henry de Lacy, first Duke of Lancaster, who paved the Long Causeway to Burnley in 1355 and had this track cut across the moor to get at a vein of lead on Stansfield Moor. Its position is still marked on the Ordnance Survey Map some 650 years later although it would be hard to find on the ground. You can see two ruined farms upstream from Colden Water. These are called Pad Laithe and Noah Dale. The lead mine was in the clough that runs to the left of Noah Dale.

Continue along Dukes Cut for about 20 minutes. At first, we are going uphill, but once up you can see the directional array at Pole Hill, which is a radio beacon for aircraft. Soon you can see the outline of the rocks at Bride Stones and Staups Moor comes into view backed by Stoodley Pike in the distance. Pass a large area on the left that has been excavated for a proposed motor cycle track! Soon you reach the road called the Long Causeway, again first paved by Henry de Lacy.

From the end of Dukes Cut walk to the right, past the end of Eastwood Road. You will soon see the Sportsman's Arms ahead on the right. **However, your route is the footpath on the left, just before the pub. This follows an old wall across Bride Stones Moor.** There is plenty of discarded sheep wool on this moor. A few local people collect it, wash, spin, dye it and then knit it into jumpers! **Keep the wall on your right and follow it until it peters out before a large rock. At this point go half-right downhill, across some rough grass, towards the unoccupied Bride Stones Farm. Before you reach the track to the farm, follow the wall on this side of it downhill, keeping it on your right.**

Ahead lies Great Hill across the valley and to its right is Flower Scar and Heald Moor leading on to Thieveley Pike – a great view of upland farms and moors. **At the bottom of the moor you go through a narrow stile and, at the end of the next field, join Stoney Lane. Turn left past the ruined cot-**

tage called Springs. You can soon hear the springs bubbling out of the hillside. Shortly after Springs you meet the Calderdale Way coming up from Todmorden. **Continue in the same direction, through the gates onto Whirlaw Common. At this point it becomes downhill all the way**.

Follow the causeway, winding across the common. As you cross, the centre of Todmorden comes into view. The lead roof of the Town Hall stands out behind the railway viaduct. Towards the end of the causeway Stoodley Pike can be seen across the valley. At the end of the common, the ruin on your right is West Whirlaw, once a pub on this old route to Burnley. East Whirlaw still stands as the next farm on your right. **After East Whirlaw the track turns right**. You soon have woods on your right which end when you reach the top of Hole Bottom Road, marked as a link path to Todmorden. **Follow the link path downhill**.

The track twists and turns, never far away from the stream and goes past some beautiful homes, old and new, in Hole Bottom Road. Todmorden is soon in sight. **At the Fountain Inn turn right down Victoria Road. Once under the railway bridge, take the first left along Railway Street. After you pass Hawthorn Place cross Wellington Road into Stansfield Road and go down it past the fire, ambulance and bus stations to reach Burnley Road. Go left here, past Todmorden Market to the Town Hall**. The Tourist Information Centre is just across the road at 15, Burnley Road.

Walk No. 8

Hebden Bridge to Todmorden via Eaves Wood, Popples Common, the Pennine Way, Gorple, Black Hameldon and Whirlaw.

Distance: 14 miles. Walking time: 7 hours. A high route.

This is a very long walk covering a lot of rough moorland. It can be exhilarating on a long summer day but it would not be sensible to choose it in winter or when there is fog or rain around. There is a chance of a lunch stop at the Pack Horse Inn, five miles into the journey, but that still leaves nine miles after lunch! In winter it would be dark long before you could finish the walk.

From Hebden Bridge Tourist Information Centre cross Bridge Gate and New Road to go down Holme Street past the Post Office and Hebden Bridge Little Theatre to reach the canal towpath. Go right past Blackpit Lock and Hebble End, under the bridge and past two locks at Stubbings. Look out for a path on your right. It is about twenty paces after milestone No. 6. Pass the cottage at Stubbing Square on your left, cross the footbridge over the River Calder and follow Colden Water upstream to the main road.

Cross the main road to Church Lane. Once past the church bear right, cross over the river and 40 yards past the bridge take the road which cuts back up right and then go round the left hairpin into the bottom of Eaves Wood. Follow the bottom path past two gates when you are above the red brick houses in Eaves Avenue. You pass one or two garages at the bottom of the wood and then begin to climb. As the tree canopy thins, dappled sunlight falls on to last year's leaves. Through the trees we get out first glimpse of Lumb Bank, once the home of Sylvia Plath and Ted Hughes, the late Poet Laureate. The house now belongs to the Arvon Foundation, whose objective it is to help creative writers.

As you reach the house, go up past Lumb Bank Cottage to the road from Heptonstall, cross it and go straight ahead. At the top of the first rise you join the Calderdale Way for about 150 yards until you come to a junction of five paths, where you take the right bridleway, with a limestone chipping surface, that climbs towards Popples Common.

At the common, turn left passing the long buildings at Black Dyke, and then turn right to the road. Go straight across the road and follow the footpath that goes across to the far wall. Where paths divide, go right. At the wall, continue uphill to a seat provided by Heptonstall Parish to celebrate the Coronation of 1937 – a place to pause and take in the landscape. Slack Top Chapel is in the foreground and the Hebden Dale on the left. **Your route runs parallel with the valley. Start to the left as you face Popples Common**. At first you meet gorse bushes, then heather and bilberry.

The path does not climb much and is a pleasant high level route. The hay meadows below provide fragrant winter fodder for the dairy herd. Wheatears rise startled from the grass as you approach. Soon you reach a gate onto Heptonstall Moor. **Continue to follow the wall until you join the Pennine Way. Gritstone cairns now guide you as the path begins to climb. The compass bearing is about 300 but you will probably not need it**.

As you approach the top, you can see Bouldsworth Hill is ahead in the distance, Walshaw to the right and Stansfield Moor over on the left. Some excellent Pennine Way maintenance has provided four slab bridges to cross the wet patches where water begins to drain off the tops. There is another slight rise before you can see down to Lower Gorple Reservoir.

It is a good time to take stock of the route ahead when you can see the whole of the reservoir. Your route will go down to the waterman's house on this side of the reservoir, then across the dam and past four conifer plantations as you climb the valley to Higher Gorple Reservoir. You can see the dam in the distance and behind it is a group of stones called Hare Stones. This is also on your route that climbs left along the top of the hill called Black Hameldon. To the right of the reservoir you can see a long low white building, probably with cars parked outside it. This is the Pack Horse Inn, also known as the Ridge, after its geographical location. There is a diversion to the pub, which will take 35 minutes, if you want to make it.

The path down off Heptonstall Moor is well marked and takes you to a bridleway coming over from Colden. When you reach it, turn right and go down to the waterman's house at Lower Gorple. When you go through the gate onto the reservoir road this is the start of the diversion. Take it from me the diversion is well worth it, as the Pack Horse is an excellent pub serving lunches from 12 till 2 on weekdays in the summer and all the year round at weekends. If you do not want to take this diversion, move on to the next paragraph. **The diversion follows the Pennine Way downhill straight ahead, where you soon pick up an old causeway that takes you down to two bridges. Cross them and follow the path left to a little gate. Beyond the gate climb to a stile on the right, marked 'pub'! Cross the field to the road and the pub is on your right. Retrace your steps after lunch**.

Go past the waterman's houses at Lower Gorple and cross the reservoir dam, then turn left and follow the double tracked road up the valley. Once, when I was walking this route, a dozen black headed gulls repeatedly dived at me, believing I was too close to their nests. You soon pass a conifer plantation and then reach a wooden hut on your right. This hut is at the junction of several paths. **Our route is straight ahead** but it is worth looking at the path across the stream which goes to the ruin you can see at Rastrick Greave, from there you can go over the moor to Noah Dale. **Continue along the road, past another plantation until you can see the dam of Higher Gorple Reservoir**. The rocky outcrop ahead is called Gorple Stones. **Cross the bridge by the end of the dam and follow the path signed to Worsthorne**.

Walking by the side of the water, with the long back of Black Hameldon in the background, you can pick out the path as it climbs to the ruined farm at Gorple, the old farm that gave its name to many of the places round here. As you reach the farm it is hard to imagine that potatoes were once grown here. **The road beyond the farm rises to the bridleway from Widdop to Worsthorne. Go left past Gorple Stones, and as you reach the top of the hill, Cant Clough Reservoir can be seen. At the top you are on the boundary where there is a Burnley Way sign and a Calderdale sign. Turn left here and follow the path to Hare Stones.** If you start to go downhill on the bridleway, you have missed the turn off.

Hare Stones is an old name for boundary stones. **Beyond Hare Stones the path drops to the col and then starts to climb Black Hameldon. The path is quite well marked on the ground at first but is easily missed on the top**. Once you have stopped climbing, you should be able to see the triangulation point in the distance for most of the time, except when you are in a hollow. **Rules here are: aim for the top, or use a compass bearing of 190. At the triangulation point the track changes direction, half left, and begins to follow a gully that goes down to Wolf Stones. After Wolf Stones, the route is still downhill to pick up the Long Causeway from Burnley at the county boundary.** You may be surprised to see a welcome to Calderdale but you have been following the boundary all the way from the Worsthorne bridleway.

As you reach the road, turn left and follow it for a quarter of a mile to Mount Lane. It is as well to face oncoming traffic, as drivers tend to speed along here. Turn down Mount Lane and look out for Lower Mount Farm on your right. **Take the bridleway on the left opposite this farm**. Note the old cross in the field on your left, just before the power lines.

This is Mount Cross, probably twelfth century, and is one of six crosses that used to mark the long causeway from Burnley to Kebcote. t is not in its original position. Norman Greenwood, one time landlord of the Sportsman's Arms was told that his grandfather had moved it. The Greenwoods have lived on this hillside for hundreds of years. The cross was called "Th' Idle God" by the locals and it was in this position on a map of 1841, so it must have been an older relative that moved it. The cross was repaired in 1895, and the annals of Halifax Antiquarian Society recount that two copper dowels now fasten the head to the upright. The base of the upright is chamfered to fit a typical base stone. The cross is leaning rather precariously and I think that it needs straightening but the experts might disagree.

The bridleway takes you to Lower Intake farm, pass behind it keeping buildings on your right. The bridleway undulates towards Todmorden passing through ten gates. The line of the walled bridleway can be seen ahead, passing to the right of Whirlaw Stones. Before you reach the fourth gate the centre of Todmorden can be seen. Soon you pass a ruined cottage called Springs – and you can hear the water bubbling out of the hill.

Shortly after Springs you meet the Calderdale Way coming up from Todmorden. **Continue in the same direction, through the gates onto Whirlaw Common.** At this point it becomes downhill all the way. Follow the causeway, winding across the common. As you cross, the centre of Todmorden comes into view. The lead roof of the Town Hall stands out behind the railway viaduct. Towards the end of the causeway, Stoodley Pike can be seen across the valley. At the end of the common, the ruin on your right is called West Whirlaw, and was once a pub on this old route from Burnley. East Whirlaw still stands as the next farm on your right. **After East Whirlaw the track turns right**. You soon have woods on your right that end when you reach the top of Hole Bottom Road, marked as a link path to Todmorden. Turn right and follow it downhill.

The track twists and turns, never far away from the stream and passes some beautiful homes, old and new, in Hole Bottom Road. Todmorden is soon in sight. **At the Fountain Inn turn right down Victoria Road. Once under the railway bridge take the first left along Railway Street. After you pass Hawthorn Place cross Wellington Road into Stansfield Road and go down it past the fire, ambulance and bus stations to reach Burnley Road. Go left here, past Todmorden Market to the Town Hall**. The Tourist Information Centre is just across the road at 15, Burnley Road.

Walk No. 9

Todmorden to Hebden Bridge. via Cross Stone, Eastwood, Jumble Hole and Rawtonstall.

Distance: 5.5 miles. alking time: 2-3hours. A low route.

From Todmorden Town Hall follow the Burnley Road past the market, under the railway viaduct, past the bus station and turn right up Stansfield Road, which you should follow to the top. At the T-junction with Wellington Road turn right and cross the railway footbridge to Stansfield Hall Road. As you reach the road, turn right and cross over. When you reach the walls around Stansfield Hall take the steps up to The Mount on your left. It is quite a pull and care is sometimes needed due to dead leaves on the steps. At the top continue upwards, past six houses on the left, and then go straight ahead into a path lined on both sides with hawthorn. The path emerges onto Cross Stone Road, which you should follow uphill, past the Old Vicarage to the top of the hill. Here you take the right fork and go between the old church and the Berghof Brandstatter Hotel and Restaurant.

Note the house on the right after the church. The top left hand room used to be Cross Stone School and the room underneath the Cross Stone Jail. The right hand end was the schoolmaster's house. Note the stocks in the wall backing on to the church. At this point you are following the edge of the valley with good views over to Stoodley Pike. You pass a colourful garden at Hollins Hall before you reach the next house on the right. This is Bean Hole Head, distinguished by its flagpole. When the barn was converted into a house some years ago the remains of an old cross was taken out of the wall and mounted in the porch. This may be the original cross of Cross Stone. The door of the old house carries the inscription RAS 1638 above the door. The chimney-breast projecting into the road contains a beehive oven.

Take the bridleway on the right immediately after Bean Hole Head. This is a pleasant route gently dropping down a wooded track. In spring, wild flowers line the banks and you eventually pass Clough Cottage down on your right. This is one of many cottages in Todmorden which does not have a road to it! It gets a little wet as you cross the Clough. **You emerge onto Matthew Lane, which is a stone covered track. Go left here for about sixty-five paces to a little wooden gate at a stile on your right**.

A depressed path follows the wall straight across three fields. You may come across a herd of Welsh Black cattle. You may be surprised to see as many bullocks as cows amongst them – and, depending what time of year it is, there may be plenty of young calves among them. This herd has lived on this land for forty years to my knowledge and they are quite docile, although they may be curious. **In the fourth field, as you start to go down to the clough, the right of way leaves the wall and bears left towards a large beech tree**. This field is wonderful in June. It has never had any weed killer on it and the wild flowers are much the same as they have been for centuries – a sight rarely seen these days. **As you reach the tree, the path follows the fence down to the left to a new footbridge across Ingham Clough**. This is a pleasant spot. Wild violets grow hereabouts, bluebells abound and rabbits scamper away on your approach.

This bridge is a bonus. Workmen had intended to replace the next one downstream but they put it in the wrong place! When the boss came to have a look at the intended bridge it was not there – so they put another one in the right place The path beyond the bridge was once little used, and it is still overgrown in parts and could do with a bit of maintenance. **Eventually it joins a green lane running past an old farm, Pex Tenements, on your right. Don't turn down to the farm but follow the green lane to the next house. At the farm track go straight across and up the green lane, which passes to the left of the row of cottages known as Chapel Houses. When you reach the back of Chapel Houses take the steps up to the right and follow the fence to a stile in the corner of the field. An old causeway path crosses the next four fields, mostly buried under the grass, and ends at Eastwood Lane**.

Eastwood is the old hamlet to your right. It once housed a water-powered mill. The duck pond was the millpond and this was fed from Staups Dam, which is behind Great Rock, up to your left. The dam is now being developed as a fish farm. At **Eastwood Lane go left, then right, following the private road to Upper House and beyond**. These houses were once run down farms but now have thankfully been restored and improved to the extent that they look neat and well kept but still in their rural setting.

Eventually the track turns into a green lane, now scattered with old vehicles. Ahead lies the valley called Jumble Hole Clough, which you have to cross. Looking half-right, you can see Hebden Bridge in the distance. Across the valley, at about the same height you can see the line of the low-level route on the south side of the valley. You are getting into bilberry country here. **The route turns uphill to a track that goes down to Roundfield Farm. You need to go behind the farm so you need to continue uphill for about 100 yards to a stile on the right. The path down is quite steep and uneven so care is needed**. Long trousers are useful as the path passes through bracken, heather and bilberries. As you go through the next stile, the sound of water tumbling over rocks grows louder. **You cross two tracks that follow the valley sides and go straight down to a lovely old slab bridge**. The peat coloured water coming down from Staups Moor once powered several mills in this valley.

When climbing out of the valley, keep to the left at first. Several paths diverge from the bridge and it is easy to take the wrong one, particularly if there is a good waymark sign at the start. You soon see a wooded bank ahead with a path that that goes through it. Before you reach the trees, turn right up the broader track, which has a wall on the high side. As you reach level ground there are great views of Jumble Hole, Stoodley Pike and the sweep of the Calder Valley. What a great place to live!

As you reach the next farm, Dove Scout, the path is to the left. Go through the two little gates and then the five-barred gate. Just after the five barred gate take the stile on the right onto a path that follows the wall along the contours. Pass behind the next farm and continue to follow the path along the wall. Overhead power lines mark the route. There are old causeway stones under the grass here, which lead to Winters Lane. As you emerge, the Pennine Way sign is just behind you.

On Winters Lane go past Long Hey Top and then straight ahead. Do not take the right path, which descends to the valley bottom. **The lane goes past two farms and then a**

Roundfield Farm nestles in Jumble Hole, with Dove Scout on the left and Hebden Bridge in the distance.

gate ahead leads to a green lane, which in turn leads to the hamlet of Rawtonstall. As you approach Rawtonstall there is a good view of Horsehold across the valley with Hebden Bridge is to the left of the television mast. Rawtonstall, once almost deserted, is now looking very well cared for. This is an old settlement recorded in the Doomsday Book as having a vinery, probably on the south bank facing the sun. **You pick up a driveable track at Rawtonstall**, which soon begins to lose height. Which is just as well because there is a lot of height to be lost to get down to Hebden Bridge! You soon see the tower of Heptonstall Church half left.

You are now dropping through a mixed wood of silver birch, holly and oak as the track goes down to a tarmac road. You can take the path to Glen View Road via Cat Steps. These are fairly steep and sometimes slippery but it is an interesting set of steps, which have recently been cleaned up, and waymarked. **I think it is safer to follow the track to the road. On reaching the road, follow it down past the eight houses at Glen View then take the steps on the right before the next houses to cut off the corner at Heath Bank. The road continues down past the church dedicated to St James the Great to join the main road at Bank Foot.**

You could follow the main road into Hebden Bridge, (the Fox and Goose Pub is just past the traffic lights). **I prefer to cross the road and take the path to the right of Colden Water, crossing the river Calder at the footbridge and going straight on to the canal towpath. You turn left and pass two locks at Stubbing, go under the next bridge**, where there is a café at Hebble End open on Fridays, Saturdays and Sundays, **on to Blackpit Lock. Here you turn left passing Hebden Bridge Little Theatre and the Post Office to arrive at New Road.** If you want a bus to Todmorden they are leave every half-hour from the bus stop on your right. The route to the railway station through Calder Holmes Park is signed.

Walk No. 10

Todmorden to Hebden Bridge. via Lobb Mill, Harvelin Park, Edge End Moor and Horsehold.

Distance: 5.5 miles. Walking time: 2-3 hours. A low route.

From Todmorden Town Hall follow Halifax Road and take the second street on the right, Union Street South, to Shop Lock on the canal, turn left and follow the old tow-path with Stoodley Pike in view. The canal is home to ducks, geese and moorhens. On the left bank we have some of Todmorden's industrial region but walls or trees often shield it. Passing under the first bridge, the new Baltimore Marina is a mooring point for the many pleasure barges, which now ply the canal. As the canal sweeps to the left, a view of the wooded hillside on the south side opens up.

The canal is a favourite haunt of fishermen. Indeed the only person I met when I did this walk was a solitary angler. The station numbers of Todmorden Angling Society count down as you walk towards Hebden Bridge. Soon you see the new houses on the south bank with their gardens that sweep down to the water's edge. At Old Royd Lock No. 17 the chimney of the Woodhouse Mill comes into view. This was built in 1832 and was going to be restored as a textile museum when it caught fire. In May this area is ablaze with banks of rhododendrons. Opposite Woodhouse Mill the river Calder comes into view and you can see how the canal, the river, the road and the rail-way compete for flat land at the valley bottom. The rugged stones of a dramatic old quarry tower above the south bank. **Soon you reach the fourth canal bridge at Lobb Mill which is where we leave the towpath.**

Lobb Mill was demolished in the 1930s. The buildings that remain were once at the gate house and one of them has become Lobb Mill Chandlers where bargees can buy new rope, batteries and other essentials of canal life. For walkers, ice cream is available and you may also see some of my postcards that illustrate the countryside around Todmorden.

At Lobb Mill leave the towpath, go over the bridge and start to climb the lane that goes up to Haugh Barn. Views of the valley quickly open up to the left and you can see

Lobb Mill, the site of a mill long gone, where the road, railway and canal wind through the S-shaped valley between Todmorden and Hebden Bridge.

how the valley follows an S-shape. Ahead you see a farm just below the skyline. This is Height Farm, which you will pass in about one hour! **As you reach the restored Haugh Barn, leave the road and take the grass track to the right**, which climbs along the edge of the wood. It can be muddy here after rain. Occasional steps take you higher until you are level with Rodwell End hamlet on the opposite side of the valley. You pass through a small gate and continue climbing until you reach the edge of the valley. **Go through a stone stile, which has a wooden fence across it, and follow the old causeway stones to Shaw Farm**. There may be an electric fence across your path but you can undo the orange insulators, pass through and replace them. The last part of the path can be muddy. The orange windsock is for a helicopter-landing pad in the farmyard. If you see it coming, stay out of the way! Dogs are usually on guard but they are chained. **Keep the buildings on your right and leave the farm at the electrically operated main gate**. Press the button and it opens, walk through and it closes. Such luxury!

When you reach the road, turn left and go past Shaw Cottage to the next road junction. Here you keep right, ignoring the sign to Hebden Bridge that points downhill. **Follow the road round to the left** where you come across Harvelin Park – a relatively new housing development. **The route ahead is straight on, following the wall on your left**. Across the valley the high point is Staups Moor which glows with heather in August. There are some lovely old farms on your left. You will pass Causewayside, Fielden House, and Middle Stoodley. This part of the route is a public bridleway. To your right, below Stoodley Pike there are some deserted farms which are gradually being bought and restored.

About 100 yards after Middle Stoodley, go straight on at the junction to Height Wood. Cross the stream at the stepping stones and follow the bridleway until it joins a farm road at a bend. Continue following this track all the way to Height Farm. Ignore a tempting white gate at a bend and keep to the track, which doubles back so that Stoodley Pike is now behind to your left. **Pass in front of Height Farm and continue straight on, through a gate to the next farm, which is called Height Gate**. The gate refers to the gate onto the moor so you will be at the top end of the agricultural plane. **Pass Height Gate, now being restored, on your left. The track**

ahead, curves left and you reach the aforesaid gate.

At this point the map shows three tracks. **Take the middle one that does not follow either wall but climbs slightly to the right.** Someone has kindly marked the route by painting occasional stones white. The track curves until you reach two old stone gateposts on the hillside at the back of Higham (which means 'high home'). At this point you are at the summit of this walk although there are a few undulations ahead. **About a hundred paces after these gateposts there is a standing stone on the right. This marks the point where your path leaves the descending green lane and branches to the right following the contours of the hill.** In spring there is lots of hawthorn blossom hereabouts and rabbits play among the grasses. **Keep your height and go through a stone stile to the right of a rather obvious water tank.** High on the hillside each old farm had its own water supply. The water is still collected, has the sediment removed and is then filtered until it meets the required standards.

The path keeps on the same level above the fence and wall on the downhill side. In the valley bottom you can see the water treatment works at Sandbed, where the river Calder deposited a bed of sand some three feet deep. From late spring into summer this is the land of skylarks and moorland birds along Edge End Moor. Soon the tower of Heptonstall Church appears in the distance across the valley. **Here you take the higher path, which keeps above the ruins of Crutonstall**, a name that denotes great age, as in Heptonstall and Rawtonstall. Soon you reach tractor tracks, which travel between Crutonstall and Edge End Farm. **Follow this track until it turns up to the farm, then continue straight ahead following the wall down to the trees.** Ahead you can see Horsehold half left where you will soon be. Up on the skyline half right is the outline of Rake Head Farm on the edge of Erringden Moor.

Soon you reach a farm road, which is part of the Pennine Way. No Pennine Way for us though. **Go straight across the road, down to an old packhorse bridge and through the gate. Keep left after the gate.** These old meadows are full of celandine in spring and then the other wild flowers follow in due season. **The route follows the top edge of Callis Wood**, which is full of bluebells and wild garlic in the spring. Cross a stream, which tumbles out of an old stone drain in the wall then crashes down the wood to the canal below. Soon you reach the cobbled road below Horsehold.

Follow this road downhill with good views of Heptonstall across the valley. About 250 yards down this road, just after where the tarmac starts, there is a little gate on the left which leads along to the seat on Horsehold Crag. The seat is welcome and has a splendid view. Colden Valley curves below Heptonstall and as it disappears, you can just see Lumb Bank, once the home of Ted Hughes, former Poet Laureate, and greatly admired in these parts. Below, backing onto the canal is the Stubbing Wharf. Ted has a poem called the Stubbing Wharf in his book "Birthday Letters" in which he recalls the feelings of his wife when he brought her to this part of the world. Close by the seat on Horsehold Crag you will find a circular hole, which is used to hold a cross at Eastertide.

Walk back to the road and go steadily downhill. This bit is hard on the knees but there is a seat further down presented by the Hepton Gala Committee in 1972.

Continue downhill, ignoring the road to Old Chamber, to the junction with Palace House Road. Cross the canal bridge, get onto the towpath, and follow it to the left. Pass the junction of the rivers Hebden and Calder to the lock at Blackpit No. 9. Turn left here past Hebden Bridge Little Theatre and the Post Office until you reach the end of the walk at the junction with New Road. The bus stop for Todmorden is just on your right. The Tourist Information Office is over the road at No. 1 Bridge Gate. There are many cafes and pubs, catering for all tastes in Hebden Bridge but my choice was the White Lion – straight along Bridge Gate, with six real ales, two lagers and good food.

Walk No. 11

Todmorden to Hebden Bridge via Lumbutts, Mankinholes, London Road, Pinnacle Lane and Fairfield.

Distance: 5.5 miles. Walking time: 2-3 hours. A medium route.

From Todmorden Town Hall follow Halifax Road to the second street on the right, Union Street, to join the canal towpath. Walk to the left and leave the towpath at the second bridge onto Key Sike Lane. Cross the bridge and take the path on the left on the high side of the canal, Kilnhurst Avenue. The white railings are your guide until they run out when you go right up to the next road, which is Summerville Road. Follow it to the left, through a group of new houses to a footpath that runs between numbers 47 and 62 at the end.

You are now on agricultural land. **The path keeps at the same level and runs to a stone stile in the far wall. Cross the first stream by the gate and go diagonally left to the next stile and to the stone bridge across the next stream. The path beyond the bridge was very overgrown when I last walked it but it keeps close to the left fence and then goes between stone walls, with the house on the left, to join Woodhouse Road. Here you turn right and then take the Calderdale Way link path just before Cherry Tree Cottage. This is a cinder track. At the first corner go straight on to the path that follows a post and wire fence**. Do not take the link path that climbs to the left.

The area to the right is a reclaimed landfill site. Note the ventilation shafts to let the methane out! As you climb, take a moment or two to rest and look back across to the Cross Stone hillside and the folding hills of Burnley Valley. **Soon the path leaves the line of the fence and climbs to the left. At this stage our route is up**. At the top you can see the square tower of Lumbutts Mill that once housed three water wheels, one above the other, and the spiral staircase that looks rather like a chimney.

Drop down to a tall stone stile in the next wall. Beyond this, the path keeps to the right of the wall at first and then switches to the left until you reach the farmyard. Follow the

A rather unusual six tank water trough at Mankinholes.

green path and the cobbled yard until you emerge in front of the Top Brink. At the far side of the Inn, just to the left of the top car park, is a stile that leads to a flagged causeway that crosses the field to Mankinholes. You come out opposite the Youth Hostel. Go right here for about 200 yards until you pass six old water troughs that are usually brim full and running over. Just past the troughs, take the bridleway on the left which is signed to Hebden Bridge.

This is London Road! The tradition hereabouts is to name roads after the place that they lead to, but I doubt many people have gone to London this way. Stoodley Pike is on the skyline ahead. You soon go through a gate on to Langfield Common and follow the rough track with a wall on your left. You can hardly get lost here, and when you can see over the wall, the views are good. The hill in the distance, behind Cross Stone Church, is Thieveley Pike. Eventually you meet a track coming up from Harvelin Park on the left and a footpath going straight up to the Pike on your right. This is part of the Todmorden Centenary Way – but it is too steep for my old legs. **Go straight on following the wall** which was rebuilt some years ago as part of dry stone walling classes. Eventually you leave the header walls of the enclosed land behind as you steadily climb the open hillside until the wind farm at Ovenden comes into view half left.

The track goes through a second gate and then is crossed by the Pennine Way coming down from Stoodley Pike. **You go on to the next gate at Swillington**. This is the highest part of this walk. It is a gradual descent from now on. At the next junction of farm tracks go straight across in the general direction of Heptonstall Church. **Once past Mittons Farm and Cottage and Higher Rough Head Farm, look out for the next, Kilnshaw Farm. This is not signed but there are four sycamore trees opposite it. At this point, leave the track, which was getting a bit unexciting, and go through the gate on the left. The path crosses three fields. These are hay meadows, so keep to the wall on the left. There is an old causeway here but most of it is buried.**

You emerge onto a green road, which is called Pinnacle Lane. Follow it to the right. There may be gates across to allow cattle free access from one side to another, but our route is straight ahead. Part of Pinnacle Lane is quite wet until you reach Pinnacle Farm on the left. Here the road becomes useable for cars. You are now in the agricultural plain above the valley, a land of sheep and skylarks. The cluster of houses at Horsehold is half left.

At the end of Pinnacle Lane, cross the road and take the footpath signed to Hebden Bridge via Weasel Hall. This path follows the wall across five fields and by the time you reach the third field Hebden Bridge is revealed before you. After the fifth field; cross the track into Crow Nest Wood. Keep close to the left wall as you make your way down. It is quite steep in parts and care is needed. As you emerge from the wood, take the walled lane down to the right. Once you get below the power lines you have an unobstructed view of Hebden Bridge. I have taken many a photograph for the Hebden Bridge Calendar from this spot.

At the bottom of the green lane go left down onto Palace House Road. There are two alternative endings here.

FIRST ALTERNATIVE: **If you want to go to the railway station follow the road to the right, at the end take the track left under the railway bridge and then climb left to the station**.

SECOND ALTERNATIVE: **Go left, cross the railway bridge and, before you reach the next houses, take the footpath on your right down to the canal bank. Cross the bridge by the Little Theatre and pass the Post Office to New Road**. The bus stop for Todmorden is on your right. The Tourist Information Centre is just on your left across the road and there are plenty of shops, cafes and pubs if you need them.

Walk No. 12

Todmorden to Hebden Bridge via Cross Stone, Great Rock, Blackshaw Head, Hebble Hole, and Heptonstall.

Distance: 7.5 miles. Walking time: 4 hours. A medium route.

From Todmorden Town Hall follow the Burnley Road past the market, under the railway viaduct, past the bus station and turn right up Stansfield Road, which you should follow to the top. At the T-junction with Wellington Road, turn right and cross the railway footbridge to Stansfield Hall Road. As you reach the road, turn right and cross over. When you reach the walls around Stansfield Hall take the steps up to The Mount on your left. It is quite a pull and care is sometimes needed due to dead leaves on the steps. At the top continue upwards, past six houses on the left, and then go straight ahead into a path lined on both sides with hawthorn. The path emerges onto Cross Stone Road, which you should follow uphill, past the Old Vicarage to the top of the hill.

At the top of the hill turn left before you reach the Berghof Brandstatter. You are soon passing Broad Gate and Todmorden Golf Club on your left, but look out for a small stone and opening into the meadow on your right. This is one of the old paved causeways that went from farm to farm. **It crosses four fields**, used for silage and sheep, so keep to the wall on the right. **You are soon approaching the barn at Lower Ashes. Keep all the buildings on your right**. Note the date-stone, 1759, and **then turn left up Ashes Lane** to the next group of houses at Higher Ashes. Note the old single storey cottage dated 1714, now used as a stable. **Continue uphill to Broad Ing Top** (the name means the top of the broad meadow). **As the track turns into the farm, take the bridleway on the right to meet the Calderdale Way crossing from left to right. Go up the steps to the right to follow the Calderdale Way** for a few miles. This is the best maintained, and signed footpath in Calderdale and a credit to the Countryside Unit which looks after it. You soon reach a vantage point on Law Hill. The quarry below was the source of stone for all the farms you see below. It was usual to cut and dress the stone in the quarry before it was taken downhill to the building site on a horse-drawn sledge. The view from Law Hill has been virtually unchanged for three hundred years apart from the power lines and recent tree planting. You see the gently sloping agricultural land, above the V-shaped valley, with the moorland beyond. The dry stone walls are a result of the Enclosure Acts.

From Law Hill, follow the path to an old road, go downhill for a few paces until the footpath continues on your left along the line of a wall. You have level going for a while past Killup Farm and Cottage, along to Butts Lane, with Butts House to your right. Cross Butts Lane, the top half of which is only passable with difficulty, and follow the path around the hill to cross Great House Clough. Just over the stream you are diverted up behind Higher Birks to pick up the green track rising beyond it.

The track turns uphill and joins Upper Lane which you should follow to the right. At this point it is well worth a look back, with a fine view of the farms on the tops, the wooded valley which carries road, rail and canal, and then the moors beyond to Stoodley Pike. The final section of Upper Lane has had its dry stone walls rebuilt during the government's Community Programme of the 1980s.

When you reach the top of Crossley New Road, known locally as the Long Drag, go left up the road and then turn right along Eastwood Road to Great Rock. Just before the rock, turn left and follow the green road. When you reach a good stone take-off, there is a building on the right, which is planned to be used for a fish farm, utilising the waters of Staups Reservoir. As you reach stile onto the moor it is worth a look around. Hebden Bridge can now be seen in the distance. To its left, the tower of Heptonstall Church is a landmark for miles around and this walk passes close to it. The route ahead follows the line of farms leading up to Blackshaw Head.

Staups Moor is a blaze of purple in August. **The path is well marked but you need to pick your way over gritstone rocks towards a tall wooden stile beyond an old bridleway**. Just before you reach it, a plank bridge crosses the goit that collects water from the moor, to fill Staups Reservoir. The moor is home to moorland birds, and in summer you will hear skylarks, wheatear, snipe, curlew, peewits but not many grouse. As you cross the stile, Hippins Farm is half-right. **There is a way-**

mark post ahead where the path drops down to Hippins Bridge. Note the new wall on the right of the bridge. This had to be rebuilt in 1999 following heavy rain that washed the road away. Hippins is an old Yorkshire name for stepping-stones. The bridge was built in 1883, replacing the hippins.

Once over the bridge, turn right and pass in front of Hippins Farm, a lovely old building built in 1656, replacing an earlier timber framed house. At the end of the farm, ignore the kissing gate on the right and **bear left towards Blackshaw Head. Continue between the farm buildings to a stile. The path runs up to Apple Tree Farm. Cross the track to the next stile where the next causeway is built over a drain. Keep the next house on your left and cross two fields to a farm track that goes up to Badger Lane**.

At this point the Shoulder of Mutton is 150 yards to your left. At the time of writing, Serena and Allan will welcome you for lunches from noon on Fridays to Sundays. If you go to it, look out for the milestone to London, 206 miles, at the end of Badger Lane. Readers who read one of my earlier books "On the Tops" will realise that the quaint old Blackshaw Head Post Office has gone.

The Calderdale Way continues on the opposite side of Badger Lane crossing seven fields diagonally. By the time you reach the third field you have a panoramic view of Heptonstall Church on your right, up along Colden Valley to the hills to the left, (Black Hameldon and Bouldsworth Hill). Crossing the seventh field the far gate is painted yellow to guide you.

Across the valley, your route will go above the wood, which you can see as you approach the yellow gate. **At the gate, go down the walled track to Shaw Bottom where you go left then right onto Colden Road**. At this point the New Delight Inn is 300 yards to your left, and at the time of writing, is open all day every day.

This walk follows the Calderdale Way, signed to the right. Soon you pass the site of Hudson Mill on your left, with its now empty millpond. After the path curves, Heptonstall Church is seen again, so **look out for the route down to the river at Hebble Hole Bridge**.

Hebble hole is often used by Pennine Way walkers as a

The old slab bridge at Hebble Hole. Both the Pennine Way and the Calderdale Way cross this bridge. A pleasant spot to rest in Summer.

resting place – what could be more pleasant. **Once over the old slab-bridge, follow the causeways to the right**. The Pennine Way climbs to the left but **our route continues along the wall side into the top of Foster Wood. You do not stay in the wood for more than a few yards before a stile leads you to causeways which cross two fields diagonally**. A landmark ahead is the house with a tall chimney, seen behind some trees, which is on our route. **Soon you pass a plantation interspersed with rocks and then the join the path, going left, leading up towards two houses. At the farm lane go right, then follow the left wall, keeping the buildings on your right. Now you have more causeways down to the junction of five paths**.

At the junction, going clockwise, the first path goes up to Popples Common and onto a great ridge walk, page 45. **The second path is our route**. The third path is a continuation of the Pennine Way but involves a bit of rough clambering at the top of Eaves Wood. The fourth path goes down some lovely old steps to the site of a mill by the river. It is well worth a peek over the wall to see these, and you have just walked the fifth path!

Now take the second path, which starts between two trees, across two fields to Fields Farm. Cross the drive and continue in the same direction across two more fields to the house with the tall chimney. Cross the road and pick up the stile opposite, continuing in the same direction. At the next stile, take the left causeway, across a field which is a mass of buttercups in June, **to the road where you turn right and then take the left track to a causeway that goes past the back of the school and behind the village, coming out at Whitehall Fold**.

Go straight ahead past the very old Whitehall Farm, with an interesting plaque on the wall at the far end. **Go under the stone lintel, dated 1579**, and onto Northgate. The route I recommend will turn left here, but for the moment it is well worth going a few yards to the right to the centre of the village, coming out by the Cross Inn. Heptonstall Post Office, just down the hill, sells a guide to the village and other goodies.

From Heptonstall you can walk down Heptonstall Road following the signs to Hebden Bridge. This is the shortest route, but it is steep, and everyone says it is worse going down than coming up! There is an hourly bus service down the hill.

If you would prefer a more gentle descent, dropping down

in three stages, **start by the side of the Cross Inn and go north along Northgate**. Notice the panel on the wall on the left, opposite No. 3 Wadsworth View. This has the initials of the builder, Henry Foster, and his wife Elizabeth and is dated 1736. Next, there is an old lintel, dated 1578, with the initials of John Bentley. To the right, is the octagonal Methodist Chapel built in 1764. **As you reach Northfield, bear right and follow the lane down past three houses to Lee Wood Road. Cross it and take the bridleway to Midgehole**. There is a short cut about 100 paces down this path - just before the first take-off a path doubles back right through the woods. It does not matter if you miss it as you can **continue to a tarmac road and turn right when you reach it**.

Both the short cut and the road bring you to the same place. The tarmac ends as the wall on the left ends. **Look out for a path on the left that drops down through the woods to the next level**. The house at No.14 The Hollins comes into view and Hebden Bridge can be seen through the trees to the left. **At the X-junction, keep to the left path along to causeway stones that meet a cobbled track.**

Turn left and follow the path down to the packhorse bridge. Once over the bridge, go right, then left onto Victoria Road. Take a right turn before Valley Road and then left along Hangingroyd Lane to the end. You pass the fire station and the market. Cross the old Hepton Bridge past the Hole in the Wall Pub (the hole was caused by a cannon ball). Turn right onto Bridge Gate, and the walk ends outside the Tourist Information Centre by the traffic lights.

Walk No.13

Todmorden to Hebden Bridge via Hole Bottom, Windy Harbour, Keelham, Back of Behind, Harleywood Gate, Strines Clough, New Delight, and Colden Clough.

Distance: 7.5 miles. Walking time: 3-4 hours. A medium route.

From Todmorden Town Hall follow the Burnley Road past the market, under the railway viaduct, past the bus station and turn right up Stansfield Road, which you should follow to the top. At the T-junction with Wellington Road turn right and cross the railway footbridge to Stansfield Hall Road. As you reach the road, turn right and cross over. Before you reach the walls around Stansfield Hall, take the road up to The Hollins.

As soon as you are clear of the trees you meet a pleasing vista over the meadows to Whirlaw Rocks and to the inter-folding hills of Burnley Valley. **At the top of the first slope go left along The Hollins to the little path at the end which brings you out onto Hole Bottom Road. The route ahead is uphill**, past Oakhill and the old Hole Bottom Mill with its now shortened chimney. **Bear left at the next junction**. Soon the sound of water tumbling down the clough will greet your ears. The track swings left, then right, around a large house with chestnut and yew trees in the garden, climbing all the time. You are soon in deep shade. **You go round an S-bend before you reach the Calderdale Way**.

At the top of Meadow Bottom you cross the Calderdale Way and continue to follow the stream uphill past Latchford Cottage. You soon pick up the cobbled track leading to Greenhurst Hey, a well-proportioned house built onto a typical Pennine farm. **Take the left track through the farmyard and follow it up two fields** – along the three phase power lines. The rocky outcrop on the left is called Whirlaw Stones and the hill behind it across the valley is Flowerscar. The microwave mast ahead is connected to glass fibre cables, which feed it digital signals – a sign of the times.

Just as the track begins to turn left, you take the stile on the right. You have finished climbing for a while so it is worth looking back to see Todmorden lying at the junction of three valleys. The way ahead is to the east to Lower Winsley, which you can see at the far end of the track. Keep Cross Stone Church and Stoodley Pike on your right. This is a bridleway and horses do sometimes churn it up. **The track drops down to a stream and then rises between steep banks** of heather and bilberries. Note the new barn conversion at Higher Winsley on your left.

Wild roses grow along the old causeway. **As you reach the tarmac road, follow it past two houses, and a gateway to a third, uphill towards an old quarry. Look out for the stile in the right wall opposite Hall Stones Green Farm. Go through this stile onto a gently sloping track, past the quarry to the next stile. From here you follow the wall to Keelham Farm. Turn left up the drive, recently surfaced with limestone, to Eastwood Road. Cross the road and go through the gate opposite to a track down to a house called Back of Behind. As you approach the house the way ahead veers right, crossing two fields to the corner of the far field where it joins an old bridleway. Follow the bridleway to the right to a ruin called Copley Holme**, which used to house the waterman in charge of stored water for the water-powered mills in Jumble Hole and Eastwood.

At the ruined house turn left, cross the slab bridge and go down towards a stile that leads down some steps to a second slab bridge. Note the breached dam on the right, which once stored water for the mills. The waterman would release it into the stream for use downstream in Jumble Hole Clough. **The way ahead is across four fields to the house you can see which is called Harleywood Gate. The stiles here are in poor condition - much like the fields. As you reach the wall at the back of the house, keep all buildings on your right; follow the path out to the main drive past the red telephone box to the main road.**

At the road, cross it to face oncoming traffic and walk left for about 150 yards to the next lane on the right, opposite Lower Moss Hall. Walk up this lane and turn left at the top on Higher Back Lane. About 300 yards further on, take the gate on the right that brings you out at Strines Clough. Keep to the right of the house and take the first gate on the left. This is a continuation of the bridleway you have just come down.

You may meet a peacock around here. You are high above the Colden Valley with views all the way down to Heptonstall Church. It is good to see farm ponds around which have not been filled in. The bridleway crosses a farm track that runs behind a large building, Field Head Farm. **Turn right and follow the track past the rear of Field Head Farm**. As you turn the corner, notice the little Strines Bridge in the field half left. Pass Strines Farm, with is assorted windows of many ages and soon you are walking towards Colden School accompanied by the sound of Colden Water. The track emerges at Jack Bridge. The New Delight pub is just up to your right serving food and refreshments at reasonable prices.

Go up the road, past the New Delight, for about one hundred yards and take the bridleway on the left. This is Colden Road. The Calderdale Way comes down from the right and goes past the house that was once Hudson Mill. Note the remains of mill-ponds. Down on the left is the ancient bridge at Hebble Hole, used by both the Pennine Way and the Calderdale Way. **You continue to follow Colden Road**, now gently slopeing downhill with heather, bilberry and bracken filling the sides of the road.

Soon you pick up intermittent causeway stones and the first of twelve wonderful take-offs. These were designed to take surface water off the track to prevent it being washed away. Lumb Bank, Ted Hughes' old home, can be seen ahead on the opposite bank. "Lumb" is an old name for a chimney and there were plenty of chimneys on that bank. The mills were originally water-powered but were then converted to steam with horse drawn carts having to bring coal from Hebden Bridge along the route you are following. You meet a track coming up from one of these mills but you continue ahead downhill.

Soon you pass three houses, on the right and begin to see red brick houses through the trees on the opposite side of the valley. These are along Eaves Avenue where there was once a silk mill. **At the end of the bridleway you follow the road downhill, past the church to the main road at the bottom**.

Cross the road and take the path to the right of Colden Water, crossing the River Calder at the footbridge and going straight on to the canal towpath. You turn left and pass two locks at Stubbing, go under the next bridge where there is a cafe at Hebble End. This is open on Fridays, Saturdays and

Sundays. **Continue to Blackpit Lock. Here you turn left passing Hebden Bridge Little Theatre and the Post Office to arrive at New Road**. If you want a bus to Todmorden, they leave every half-hour from the bus stop on your right. The route to the railway station through Calder Holmes Park is signed.

Walk No. 14

Todmorden to Hebden Bridge via Longfield, Lumbutts, Stoodley Pike, Dick's Lane, Erringden Moor and Crow Nest Wood.

Distance: 7 miles. Walking time: 3-4 hours. A high route.

From Todmorden Town Hall, follow Rochdale Road for a hundred yards to the Golden Lion. Turn left, up Longfield Road, and begin the climb out of the town. Longfield Road goes left opposite number 99 and climbs round the corner to Longfield Terrace. Take the farm road to the left just before the terrace. At the next junction, take the left fork to emerge in front of Higher Longfield Farm. Just before the cattle grid, take the stile on the left and follow the path across six fields to a green lane, where you turn right to come out on Lumbutts Road. Follow the road to the left through Lumbutts Village. Go down the hill and up to the Methodist Chapel. Take the path opposite the chapel signed to Stoodley Pike.

You soon see the old causeway stones running between two walls, through a gate, and out onto the Langfield Common. **Follow these causeways to the top**. It is a bit of a pull but the views are worth it. Just before the top, the causeways take a right turn and there is a handy seat up on your left, placed there in memory of Arthur Archer, one time warden of Mankinholes Youth Hostel.

The Causeway continues over to Cragg Vale, but you **turn left at the top and follow the Pennine Way to Stoodley Pike**. Note the tall leaning stone called Long Stoop. In the old days it was decreed that stoops be set up on highways to guide the travellers over the moors. Long Stoop has survived many a year and it has been put up straight once but it is well out of the vertical now. Walking time from Long Stoop to Stoodley Pike usually takes about twenty minutes. You need to watch your feet picking their way over gritstone rocks ingrained with pebbles of silica. Just think – if these were converted to silicon chips, how many computers could you make? There are two large gritstone cairns on the way from Long Stoop to Stoodley Pike. If you stop by the second one, walk downhill a little way and you will soon spot a stack of causeway stones that were probably cut in about 1730, ready for a horse drawn sledge to take them to a construction site. They have never been used and are still there today.

Stoodley Pike is the name of the hill, although most people call the monument by that name. This is thought to be the third monument built on this site. The present one was erected at the end of the Crimean War, the previous one, which was circular in section, having been struck by lightning on the day the Russian Ambassador left London at the start of the war. The previous monument was a peace monument to mark the end of the Napoleonic War. Little is known about the earliest one, although it is known that Stoodley Pike was a beacon site and Stone Age artefacts have been found around here.

From Stoodley Pike, make towards the scots pine plantation following the Pennine Way. Note the walled green lane to the left of the plantation. This is Dick's Lane on our route ahead. On the way down from Stoodley Pike you will pass a spring on your right. This feeds a stone trough inscribed "Public slakin trough". It never runs dry even though it is only a few feet below the top of the moor. In recent years a green algae has appeared, which makes me less likely to slake my thirst there. **Thirty paces beyond the stone stile you leave the Pennine Way, which drops down to Swillington from here. Instead, you continue to follow the wall to Dick's Lane and then go left along it**. It can be wet underfoot here. Dick's Lane rises at first and then drops to Erringden Moor. As you descend, the wind farm at Ovenden can be seen again.

At the end of Dick's Lane, follow the sign to Daisy Bank along the right wall. At the end of the wall you are on open moorland. The path soon disappears and it becomes a case of choose your own. The compass bearing is about 50 degrees. There are two stone markers and, by the time you reach the second one, you can see down into Daisy Bank and Mytholmroyd. You can see Bell House Farm over on the right and Rake Head on the left.

In summer the sounds of moorland birds are never far away, anxious peewits and curlews will be sounding their alarm calls to divert attention from their nests. Little white rumped wheatears flit among the moorland grasses. Years ago one would have heard snipe, and although you still hear them occasionally, they seem quite rare now.

The ground becomes wetter towards the bottom of the moor and there is a tendency to veer to the right because you can see down the valley. This does not matter because **when you reach the far side, there is a path that returns you to the left to where you ought to be. If you see a yellow marker where a path drops down to the wood, you have gone too far to the right. Do not go down this path, but follow the path to the left along the line of an old wall and this will return you to a way-marked sign to Daisy Bank. Again, do not follow this sign, instead follow the wall to the left to the next corner and then go diagonally across to a three bar wooden stile which is your correct exit from the moor**.

It is downhill from here. **Follow the line of a sunken path to the farm track where you go left** to enjoy a gentle sheltered descent in the general direction of Heptonstall Church which you can see across the valley. The track passes two houses before arriving at Great Jumps Farm, where there is a short power pylon. **Just beyond the farm, leave the track and take the stile on the left and follow the wall across the first field to the next stile. In the second field, go diagonally right downhill towards the red brick farm building**.

At the farm, cross the track to a stile, just to the left of the sheep pen. The route here goes diagonally left, to a stile in the wall. From this point you follow old causeway stones across three fields, again in the general direction of Heptonstall Church, to a stile at the top of Crow Nest Wood. The decent through the wood can be slippery.

At the bottom of the wood, the whole of Hebden Bridge is in clear view. If you want to go to the railway station there is a short cut down the right path, under the railway bridge and up left to the station. If you want to go to the town centre **take the left track, which has changing surfaces, all the way down to Palace House Road. Turn left, cross the railway bridge and take the signed footpath on the right down the steps to the canal. Cross the bridge passing Hebden Bridge Little Theatre and the Post Office to emerge on New Road, opposite the Tourist Information Centre**. Buses to Todmorden are on your right. There are plenty of pubs and cafes offering refreshment to add to your sense of well-being after such an adventurous walk!

Lumbutts Long Causeway. Built around the year 1730, these causeways were once, highways carrying pack horses and pedestrians across the hills.

Walk No. 15

Todmorden to Hebden Bridge via Wickenberry, Kebcote, Dukes Cut, Egypt, Reaps Cross, New Delight and Colden Road.

Distance: 10.5 miles. Walking time: 4-5 hours. A high route.

From Todmorden Town Hall follow the Burnley Road past the market, under the railway viaduct, past the bus station and turn right up Stansfield Road, which you should follow to the top. At the T-junction with Wellington Road, turn right and cross the railway footbridge to Stansfield Hall Road. As you reach the road, turn right and cross over. Before you reach the walls around Stansfield Hall, take the road up to The Hollins.

As soon as you are clear of the trees you meet a pleasing vista over the meadows to Whirlaw Rocks and to the inter-folding hills of Burnley Valley. **At the top of the first slope go left along The Hollins to the little path at the end which brings you out onto Hole Bottom Road**. The route ahead is uphill, past Oakhill and the old Hole Bottom Mill with its now shortened chimney. **Bear left at the next junction**. Soon the sound of water tumbling down the clough will greet your ears. The track swings left, then right, around a large house with chestnut and yew trees in the garden, climbing all the time. You are soon in deep shade and them you go round an S-bend before you reach the Calderdale Way.

At the Calderdale Way, follow it to the left with woods on your left. Once past the woods, Whirlaw Stones can be seen ahead. Your route goes to the left of them. **At the turn off to Cally Hall Farm, go left, still following the Calderdale Way to the gate onto Whirlaw Common**. The ruined building on the left was once West Whirlaw, which used to be an ale-house on the packhorse route. When the turn-pike road was built in the valley bottom, the trade disappeared and the licence was transferred to the Bay Horse Inn at Cross Stone. This in turn was renamed the Berghof Brandstatter in 1987.

The causeway winds across the common with glorious views of Thieveley Pike, Heald Moor, Flowerscar and Great Hill. At the time of writing there are planning applications for wind farms on some of these hills. Let's hope that they keep off the skyline. The wind farm at Coal Clough ahead is quite well sited. **The causeways continue after the common to join Stoney Lane, a green bridleway that we will follow for some time**.

Some eighty paces after the second gate on Stoney Lane, the Calderdale Way drops down to Todmorden but **we continue on the same level** towards the ruin called Springs. As you pass, you will hear the sound of water coming out of the hillside.

Look out for a stile on your right. It is about forty paces beyond the stone building on your left. Go through the stile. The path climbs quite steeply at first, following the line of the wall on your left to a narrow stile at the top of the field. Once through the second stile you can see Bride Stones Farm, now unoccupied, and you are on Bride Stones Moor. When you are level with the track to the farm, your route bears right across some rough tufted grass towards the rocks.

You are looking for the remains of an old wall that starts between the first and second groups of rocks. Once found; follow this wall across the moor keeping it on your left. This area is popular with rock climbers and moorland birds. As you near the far side of the moor, you will see the green hut belonging to the local gun club, and then the white walls of the Sportsman's Arms pub and restaurant. At the time of writing, it is open all day from Friday to Sunday.

On reaching the road walk uphill, past the end of Eastwood Road, to the first bridleway on the left and follow it to Four Gates End. This track is called Dukes Cut so named after Henry de Lacy, first Duke of Lancaster, who paved the long causeway to Burnley in 1355 and had this track cut across the moor to get at a vein of lead on Stansfield Moor. Its position is still marked on the Ordnance Survey Map some 650 years later, although it would be hard to find on the ground.

The radio beacon, which you pass on your left, is one of many throughout the world, used by civil aircraft computers to guide aircraft to their pre-programmed destination. Dukes Cut has been widened in recent times and a huge car park has been excavated on the right hand side. **Continue past two ruined houses on the right** – the telephone wires still go to one of them! You know when you are approaching Four Gates End because the track starts to drop down and you can see across the moors from Black Hameldon on the left to Bouldsworth Hill and Withins Height. You can see the deserted farms on the left at Noah Dale and Pad Laithe.

When you reach Four Gates End there is now only one gate, but you can see where four tracks meet. **You take the track on the left that has been fenced off, where a stile has been provided. This follows the right hand wall down to the stream at the bottom, in the general direction of Pad Laithe.**

It is wonderful to have a right of way across such open moorland. Walking it on the longest day of the year, the moorland was in dappled sunlight and clouds raced across the sky. Curlews, skylarks and peewits were all in full cry. The water begins to collect towards the bottom of the moor and boggy bits need care. **Soon you reach an old bridge and follow the walled lane beyond to the farm track where you turn right. This takes you to the ruined farm called Colden Water.**

The track drops down to Colden Water and climbs again towards Hoar Side, the highest occupied farm in this valley. Go through the gate and before you reach Hoar Side look out for a little gate that leads to a causeway path passing below the farm. After two fields, the causeway bears left towards the next occupied farm called Egypt, crossing a bridge and a stile to join the farm track. Go past Egypt, with its newly restored barn roof, to join Edge Lane at the next gate.

At this point, you have the opportunity of a diversion onto Heptonstall Moor, which will take 25 minutes, to look at an ancient milestone to Colne and Reaps Cross, a way-marker en route to Rastrick Greave. If you don't want to see these, skip the rest of this paragraph. **Follow the permissive bridleway towards Lower Gorple and note the power line posts. At the third post, the bridleway goes left but you should follow the lines to the fifth post. Just to the west of this you will find an old causeway and a sign post marked to CLN 6 M (to Colne 6 miles).** In fact the distance is 8 miles because this post is marked in old Lancashire miles which pre-date the statute of 1594 which defined the mile. The old Lancashire mile was one and a third statute miles. There are three other milestones, marked in old miles, in Todmorden. Standing on the causeway and looking at the milestone you will see the corner of a walled field about 200 yards away. **Walk towards this corner, and as you approach**

it, you will see a standing stone just to the right of it. This is Reaps Cross. It was made in three parts. The base and bottom part have stood for many years but the top portion was fastened with metal bands and broke off. It has been lying on the ground for a long time. At the time of writing there is a plan to repair it to mark the millennium. Hopefully it will have been done by the time you read this. **Return to gate where you came onto the moor to continue**.

Follow the bridleway to Colden. The ruined farm at Lane Side on the right is typical of the state of many properties in Colden in the middle of the twentieth century but in the latter half, people have been moving back into the valley and restoring these old farms. The trees on the left around Salt Pie and Land Farm were planted in the 1970s and now provide good shelter. As you pass Longtail Cottage on your left, you can see Land Farm in the valley bottom. Its gardens are beautiful and are sometimes open to the public in summer.

At this point you have two options for the next half-mile. **You can cut down the valley just after Longtail Cottage, via the farm road going down half right. This comes out behind Colden School and you turn right to get to the New Delight.** Alternatively, it really is worth continuing along the road for a little way to Highgate Farm Shop. This is on your right opposite a small parking area. It sells everything from whisky to socks and cakes, and has been a prize winner in the best village shop competition. **At Highgate Farm, turn right into the field below the farm and walk to the stile in the bottom right corner. Follow the wall to the next farm, squeeze past the pig sty and turn left following the track down to the road where you turn right. Go past Colden School to the Smithy Bridge and the New Delight.**

Go up the road, past the New Delight, for about one hundred yards and take the bridleway on the left. This is Colden Road. The Calderdale Way comes down from the right and goes past the house that was once Hudson Mill. Note the remains of mill ponds. Down on the left is the ancient slab-bridge at Hebble Hole, used by both the Pennine Way and the Calderdale Way. **You continue to follow Colden Road**, now gently slopeing downhill with heather, bilberry and bracken filling the sides of the road.

Soon you pick up intermittent causeway stones and the

first of twelve wonderful take-offs. These were designed to take surface water off the track to prevent it being washed away. Lumb Bank, Ted Hughes' old home, can be seen ahead on the opposite bank. "Lumb" is an old name for a chimney and there were plenty of chimneys on that bank. The mills were originally water-powered but were then converted to steam, with horse drawn carts to bring coal from Hebden Bridge along the route you are following. You meet a track coming up from one of these mills but you **continue ahead downhill**.

Soon you pass three houses on the right and begin to see red brick houses through the trees on the opposite side of the valley. These are along Eaves Avenue where there was once a silk mill. **At the end of the bridleway you follow the road downhill, past the church to the main road at the bottom.**

Cross the road and take the path to the right of Colden Water, crossing the river Calder at the footbridge and going straight on to the canal towpath. You turn left and pass two locks at Stubbing, go under the next bridge where there is a cafe at Hebble End. This is open on Fridays, Saturdays and Sundays. **Continue to Blackpit Lock. Here you turn left passing Hebden Bridge Little Theatre and the Post Office to arrive at New Road**. If you want a bus to Todmorden, they leave every half-hour from the bus stop on your right. The route to the railway station through Calder Holmes Park is signed.

Walk No. 16

Todmorden to Hebden Bridge via Whirlaw Common, Black Hameldon, Gorple, the Pennine Way, Popples Common and Eaves Wood.

Distance: 14 Miles. Walking time: 7 Hours. A high route.

This is a long walk, covering miles of open moorland. It is a wonderful walk on a long summer day but is too long for a winter walk. Do not forget your compass! The Pack Horse Inn is some nine miles along the route and they do serve lunches from 12 to 2 pm on weekdays in summer and at weekends all the year round. You need an early start for this walk.

From Todmorden Town Hall follow the Burnley Road past the market, under the railway viaduct, past the bus station and turn right up Stansfield Road, which you should follow to the top. At the T-junction with Wellington Road turn right and cross the railway footbridge to Stansfield Hall Road. As you reach the road, turn right and cross over. Before you reach the walls around Stansfield Hall, take the road up to The Hollins.

As soon as you are clear of the trees you meet a pleasing vista over the meadows to Whirlaw Rocks and to the inter-folding hills of Burnley Valley. **At the top of the first slope, go left along The Hollins to the little path at the end which brings you out onto Hole Bottom Road. The route ahead is uphill**, past Oakhill and the old Hole Bottom Mill with its now shortened chimney. Bear left at the next junction. Soon the sound of water tumbling down the clough will greet your ears. The track swings left, then right, around a large house with chestnut and yew trees in the garden, climbing all the time. You are soon in deep shade and then you go round an S-bend before you reach the Calderdale Way.

At the Calderdale Way, follow it to the left with woods on your left. Once past the woods, Whirlaw Stones can be seen ahead. Your route goes to the left of them. **At the turn off to Cally Hall Farm, go left, still following the Calderdale Way to the gate onto Whirlaw Common.** The ruined building on the left was once West Whirlaw, which used to be an ale house on the packhorse route. When the turn-pike road was built in the valley bottom the trade disappeared and the licence was transferred to the Bay Horse Inn at Cross Stone. This in turn was renamed the Berghof Brandstatter in 1987.

The causeway winds across the common with glorious views of Thieveley Pike, Heald Moor, Flowerscar and Great Hill. At the time of writing there are planning applications for wind farms on some of these hills. Let's hope that they keep off the skyline. The wind farm at Coal Clough ahead is quite well sited. **The causeways continue after the common to join Stoney Lane, a green bridleway that we will follow for some time.**

Some eighty paces after the second gate on Stoney Lane, the Calderdale Way drops down to Todmorden but we **continue on the same level** towards the ruin called Springs. As you pass, you will hear the sound of water coming out of the hillside. The path descends to cross a stream. Just after the next gate, note the dry stone wall on the left. This was re-built by Tom Chapman in 1982. He was in his late seventies at the time and he wanted to leave the wall tidy before he died. Tom was a real country gentleman and his photograph remains in the Sportsman's Arms, his local, up the hillside.

At the next gate on the right, pause to look across two fields to the rocks on the skyline. Just to the right of the far gate are two rocks, spaced the width of a cottage, and indeed there used to be a cottage built between these rocks. It was called Fast Ends for obvious reasons! **Continue along the bridleway with Hudson Moor on your left.** This has an old causeway across it, now buried, to a well preserved packhorse bridge which leads to Hartley Royd, the lovely old farm which you can see across the moor. Up on the right are the rocks of Hawk Stones, well named because this area is the natural habitat of many moorland birds. You pass a new plantation of Norway spruce as you drop down to the bridge across Redmires Water. The surface of the bridleway deteriorates around here **but continue to follow it, across a bridleway junction, to pass behind the farm at Higher Intake**. Beyond the farm, note the standing stone on the skyline, in a field on the right, almost level with the power lines. Have a good look at it when you reach it.

This is Mount Cross, probably twelfth century, and is one of six crosses that used to mark the Long Causeway from Burnley to Kebcote. It is not in its original position. Norman Greenwood, one time landlord of the Sportsman's Arms, was told that his grandfather had moved it. The Greenwood family has lived on this hillside for hundreds of years. The cross was called "Th' Idle God" by the locals and it was in this position on a map of 1841, so it must have been an older relative who moved it. The cross was repaired in 1895, the annals of Halifax Antiquarian Society recounting that two copper dowels now fasten the head to the upright. The base of the upright is chamfered to fit a typical base stone. The cross is leaning rather precariously, and I think that it needs straightening, but the experts might disagree.

You soon reach Mount Lane, walk uphill to the next T- junction and walk to the left. It is as well to face oncoming traffic. Now you are on one of Todmorden's long causeways but this one is now a tarmac road. The old causeway went down the bridleway past Bank Top and Stiperden farms. In 1835 the parishes of Stansfield and Cliviger, which were responsible for highways at the time, agreed that they would no longer maintain the route past the farms but would keep to the road that followed the contour. The road was built by the Townley family in 1805, when they were enclosing land as part of the Enclosure Acts. They also built a toll-house that you can see ahead, at Stiperden Bar. The wall on the right is the wall built in 1805, and while some of it has lasted 200 years, other parts have slipped with the land. The causeway was first paved by Henry de Lacey, the first Duke of Lancaster, in 1355 because he wanted to get to a vein of lead on Stansfield Moor. He also cut a track across the moor, which is called Dukes Cut to this day.

Follow the road to the county boundary. The stream is the boundary at this point. Cross the bridge and climb onto the moor on your right. The land here belongs to Northwest Water, who have kindly granted access to this wonderful moorland. **The path is now fairly well marked on the ground** since this part of the route was described in my earlier book "On the Tops" in 1986. You still have to negotiate wet ground, but very soon you see the outline of Wolf Stones. **After Wolf Stones, the path veers left, aim for the highest ground and you will soon reach the triangulation point**.

From the summit the route is about 20 degrees east of north along a slight depression in the ground. Walk towards the summit of Lad Law in the distant background. There are some old boundary stones along the route but they are easily missed. Soon views across to Burnley and Pendle can be seen on the left as we follow a drain. This eventually goes to the left but **we continue straight on, aiming for the next summit.**

After the next summit, as you begin the descent, the depression turns to the left. Follow it down and you will soon see Cant Clough reservoir to the left. The group of rocks ahead is called Hare Stones, hare being an old word for boundary. At the bottom of the hill you can see Higher Gorple Reservoir on your right. **Climb to Hare Stones and continue climbing beyond until you meet the bridleway from Worsthorne to Widdop.**

Turn right to Widdop and, as the track climbs, look out for a built road on your right going down to the ruined farm at Gorple and follow it down. As you approach the farm you can see the outline of **the path ahead running to the left side of the reservoir dam**. The long back of Black Hameldon fills the landscape behind the water. In summer there are lots of moorland birds here, particularly curlews and peewits and you may see Canada geese on the reservoirs. At the reservoir dam, **follow the sign to Lower Gorple on the double tracked road.** The grass patch between the tracks is the best place to walk.

As you approach the first conifer wood you get a glimpse of Lower Gorple Reservoir and the Pack Horse Inn beyond it. When you pass a wooden hut, there is an interesting junction of paths, even though we are going straight on. The path across the stream goes to the ruin at Rastrick Greave and then on either to Reaps Cross or over the moor to Noah Dale.

It is good to see a new plantation with deciduous trees – rowan, birch, hazel, oak and hawthorn – to relieve the monotony of conifers. When once I approached Lower Gorple, about a dozen black headed gulls started to dive bomb me – I was too near their nests I fear. **Walk across the dam at Lower Gorple, then follow the road past the semi-detached houses until you meet the Pennine Way.**

Your route ahead will turn right up the Pennine Way but this is the closest point to the Pack Horse Inn. A diversion there will add about 35 minutes to your journey plus the time you spend there. Take it from me, the diversion is well worth it. The Pack Horse Inn is an excellent pub serving lunches from 12 till 2 on weekdays in the summer and all the year round at week-

Mount Cross, dating from the 12th Century, is one of six crosses which marked the route between Burnley and Kebcote. It is not in its original position.

ends. If you do not want to take this diversion move on to the next paragraph. **The diversion follows the Pennine Way downhill to the left, where you soon pick up an old causeway that takes you down to two bridges. Cross them and follow the path to the left to a little gate. Beyond the gate, climb to a stile on the right, marked 'pub'! Cross the field to the road and the pub is on your right. Retrace your steps after lunch.**

If you have come from the pub, go straight ahead when you reach the houses at Lower Gorple. If you have just passed the semi-detached houses, turn right and go through the gate following the Pennine Way. **Follow the Pennine Way to the next gate, then turn left along the edge of Heptonstall Moor.** The route is well marked, and as we begin to climb, a drain on the right diverts water from the path. On the top, **stone cairns mark the path** and four stone slab bridges take you over gullies where water drains from the moor.

Beyond the bridges we start to go downhill and walk towards the tower of Heptonstall Church in the distance. **The cairns guide you down to a wall, which you should follow towards the church tower** and leave the Pennine Way to climb again. Our route is down to Hebden Bridge from now on. There is a gate at the end of the moor but **your path continues in the same direction**. The vegetation changes to bilberry, heather and gorse as you approach the top of Popples Common. There is a welcome seat here, provided by Heptonstall Parish, to celebrate the Coronation of 1937.

Pause here to take stock of the way ahead. In the foreground of Heptonstall Church lies Popples Common, well used by local people for recreation. In front of the Common is the Burnley to Heptonstall road. To the right of the church is the steep slope of Eaves Wood. Your route goes down to Popples Common and then down through Eaves Wood.

From the seat, follow the wall on the left downhill and look out for a well-worn path on the right, which cuts across to the road. Cross the road and go forward to the old houses where you turn left and pass Black Dyke. Look out for the bridleway to Lumb Bank, just before the new houses. This has been dressed with limestone chippings. **As you reach a junction of five paths you join the Calderdale Way for about 150 yards, then take the path to the right, just after a large sycamore tree. The path is quite steep, with a stone gully on**

the high side. Note the red brick houses nestling at the bottom of Eaves Wood. You will soon be passing these.

Cross the road that leads to the house called Lumb Bank and follow the wall behind it past Lumb Bank Cottage. Lumb Bank was once the home of Sylvia Plath and Ted Hughes, our late Poet Laureate. It now belongs to the Arvon Foundation whose objective it is to encourage creative writing. It is a lovely spot.

You are soon in Eaves Wood, where the ground is covered in low-growing ivy. Dappled sunlight comes through the trees, shining on the old beech nuts that crunch under your feet as you go. When other paths join, **continue in the same general direction, behind the red brick houses, passing two gates until you double back to join the road. Go left, across the bridge, passing the school and the church to emerge on Halifax Road.**

Cross the road and take the path to the right of Colden Water, crossing the river Calder at the footbridge and going straight on to the canal towpath. You turn left and pass two locks at Stubbing, go under the next bridge where there is a cafe at Hebble End. This is open on Fridays, Saturdays and Sundays. **Continue to Blackpit Lock. Here you turn left passing Hebden Bridge Little Theatre and the Post Office to arrive at New Road.** If you want a bus to Todmorden, they leave every half-hour from the bus stop on your right. The route to the railway station through Calder Holmes Park is signed.

Bibliography

Boswell, Geoff, *On the Tops around Todmorden* (Delta G, 1986)
Boswell, Geoff, *Short Walks for Motorists* (Delta G, 1990)
Calder Civic Trust, *Pennine Walks Around Hebden Bridge* (1989)
Calder Civic Trust, *Heptonstall Trail* (1981)
Calderdale Way Association, *Calderdale Way Guide 3rd edition* (1997)
Dawson, W. B. *Rambles in and around Todmorden* (1932)
Hannan, Paul *Walking Country: Calderdale* (Hillside, 1996)
Heywood, M. F. and Jennings, B. *History of Todmorden* (Smith Settle, 1996)
Jarratt, Jim *The Fielden Trail, A Ramble through Todmorden's Past* (Smith Settle 1988)
Manning, John, *25 Walks in the South Pennines* (Stationery Office, 1997)
Morrison, John and Speakman, Lydia *Pennine Rails and Trails* (Leading Edge, 1990)
Spencer, Colin *The History of Hebden Bridge* (Hebden Bridge Literary & Scientific Society, 1991)

Telephone numbers of lunch stops

Many of the pubs on the routes between Todmorden and Hebden Bridge are open at lunchtimes at weekends and bank holidays but not all of them are open at lunchtimes on weekdays. If you would like to use them as a lunch stop, it is as well to telephone them the evening before to find out their opening hours. Landlords change and opening hours change to meet demand. The telephone numbers listed below were correct at the start of the year 2000, but no doubt new developments with cable and the internet will change these numbers in time.

Cross Inn, Heptonstall	01422 843833
Hinchliffe Arms, Cragg Vale	01422 325688
New Delight, Jack Bridge	01422 846178
Pack Horse, Widdop	01422 842803
Queen Hotel, Todmorden	01706 811500
Shepherd's Rest, Todmorden	01706 813437
Shoulder of Mutton, Blackshaw Head	01422 846460
Sportsman's Arms, Kebcote	01706 813449
Stubbing Wharf, Hebden Bridge	01422 844107
Top Brink, Lumbutts	01706 812696
White Hart, Todmorden	01706 812198
White Lion, Heptonstall	01422 842027
White Lion, Hebden Bridge	01422 842197

Tourist Information Centres

The Tourist Information Centres can provide details of accommodation in the area.

Hebden Bridge: Telephone 01422 843831

Todmorden: Telephone 01706 818181

Transport

Bus Times: Telephone 0113 245 7676.

Train Times: Telephone 0345 48 49 50 (24 hours)

Index